Wine Art

The Complete Wine Guide for Wine Lovers incl. Food and Wine Journal

[1st Edition]

[Pierre Laurent Bonheur]

Table of Contents

History of Wine

Vinophobia: the fear of running out of wine

What is wine?

It is grape juice that has been encouraged to ferment. Actually, it is not simply just that. Although wine may be complex, it is also practically enigmatic. Historically, wine has progressed into a symbol of hedonism and social standing. In today's world, wine is more than ever before linked with the three Fs: friends, food, and fun. Wine has for all time been regarded as among the noblest of drinks as well as proving a favourite with every type of person. Available in overwhelming varieties and flavours, wine as a drink goes down well with almost any meal or snack. What would a cheese and wine cocktail party be without it? Historically, wine is closely linked with foods, the beginnings of agriculture, and man himself. Wine has been in existence since early history of man and has persevered to be around still in modern times. Although other fermented crops, such as those used for beer, are older than grapes, wine was the more popular choice in terms of social beverages. Are you able to admit to knowing much regarding the history and origin of wine? The earliest written evidence of the cultivation of grapevines is found in the Old Testament, where it states that Noah planted his own vineyard and made wine. Scientifically, the first evidence of wine was the discovery of fossilized vines going back 60 million years. In the Middle East, wine was an accidental discovery. An ancient Persian tale tells the story of a member of King Jamshid's harem who attempted to take her own life by eating spoiled grapes from a jar after losing favour with the King. The result was an intoxicated Persian woman who became somewhat dizzy and then fell into a drunken stupor. When she awoke, it was to discover that her distress was no more. She returned to her source of relief which inevitably led to a change in behaviour, consequentially earning her the return into the King's favour. The King spread the word around court regarding his harem member's discovery and commanded an increase in spoiled grapes. Back in the day, wine was limited to be a bringer of joy to the upper class, while beer was imbibed by the working and lower classes. Quite a dilemma if you consider the well-known fact that wine drinking began as early as 6,000 BC.

Ancient History

The common perception is that early farmers 'brewed' alcoholic drinks from berries and wild fruits - including wild grapes – regardless of the lack of any written records on the pre-history of this popular beverage. Wine became easier to store when clay pots were conceived of around 9,000 years ago. The clues as to the contents of these archaeological discoveries shows small, sour type grapes, which really accounts for no particular proof of them being used to make wine. What it did do, however, was plant the notion that led to the domestication of grapes in times to come. This domestication of the grape began in the very early Bronze age in the regions of the Near East from 3200 BC. Sumer and Egypt show the most evidence of wine making going back to 3000 BC. The exact location of the first makings of wine remains a mystery, although it is most likely around the region of North Africa extending to Central and South Asia.

Ancient Greece

Wine making in ancient Greece may well have been the basis of what we know of vinification in contemporary time. Greece proves to have a great many grape varieties very similar to those grapes evidently about back in the start of civilizations. It is widely believed that today's popular Greek wine, Retsina, points to that time in history when wine jugs were lined with a certain tree resin affording the wine a distinct flavour. Archaeological digs around Greece bore the remains of a 6,500-year-old grape, which signifies the first presence of wine cultivation or growing in Europe. Semi-dehydrated gypsum was utilized before fermentation in ancient Greece, which added a form of lime to reduce the acidity. Greek wines were distributed widely in and about the Mediterranean, accounting for its eventual infiltration into early Egypt.

Ancient Egypt

In early times in Egypt, wine seemed to be very much favoured for ceremonies. The vinification industry in the Nile valley flourished in the Nile valley once grape cultivation was introduced in 3000 BC with early Bronze age trade. Wine was not only pertinent in everyday life in ancient times, but very prominent in the eternal hereafter. Wine was stored alongside other possessions in the tombs of the deceased for the purpose of enjoyment in the afterlife. Ancient Egypt saw wine red in colour due not to pomegranates as was the belief, but rather because of the red grape. It was only recently discovered that white wine was predominant in ancient Egypt too. The tomb of Tutankhamen revealed five clay amphorae or Greek jars which showed distinct traces of having stored white wine.

Ancient Rome

Romans made a significant contribution to the study of wine and the development of wine making. For the ancient Romans, wine was an integral part of a normal diet, and winemaking became a well-defined business. It is a marked fact that the major wine producing regions within contemporary Western Europe were originally established by the Romans. The expertise for viticulture improved radically with a good deal of grape varieties and cultivation techniques developed. Fine wine for which Romans were well known presumably exhibited medicinal properties when mixed with minerals and herbs. To this end it became common practice to dissolve pearls in wine before imbibing the substance. Europe declined into the Dark Ages after the fall of the Roman Empire. During this time wine production continued through the church which was the only stable structure within the society.

Middle Ages

The Middle Ages saw wine become the common drink for all the classes throughout the south. The northern locations enjoyed no grape growing at all of its own, with the most popular drinks being ale, beer, and mead, while vodka and spirits were the popular choice in the East. With wine being all important for celebrations within the Catholicism religion, it was vital for the supply to be unstaunched and continuous. Portugal is of the oldest as far as wine traditions go, and it was here that the appellation system was created for application throughout the world.

Modern World

Phylloxera adversely affected wine production and vines throughout Europe in the late 19th century, which led to the loss of many original wine varieties. Grape phylloxera is a minute aphid-like insect, smaller than a millimetre in size, that lives on and feeds off the roots of grapevines. It causes root damage which leads to the decline and eventual death of the grapevine. This phenomenon may initially have had a negatively outcome, but it eventuality did help to improve the superiority of the vineyards across Europe. It was a point in case of Darwin's theory of evolution, only as relating to wine grapes and not man. Weak varieties of grapevines perished while only the strongest survived. Latin America enjoyed their first taste of wine with the shipment of wheat and grapes by early Spanish explorers. In America today, wine is widely cultivated throughout California, Argentina, and Chile, but historically the quality was not greatly valued. Only during the late 20th century have American wines been considered anywhere as superior as the European wines.

Wine Making

It makes sense that Dionysus is not only the god of the grape-harvest, winemaking and wine, but also of fertility, religious ecstasy, ritual madness, and theatre

Wine making is a science and also a natural process which requires very little human involvement. Winemaking involves five crucial steps:

one, harvesting;

two, crushing and pressing;

three, fermentation;

four, clarification; and

five, aging and bottling.

Harvesting involves the process of picking the ideal grapes at the point when they are ready to be harvested. Determining when to harvest grapes is where the science comes in. The sweetness as well as the acidity of the wine and its flavour are dependent immensely on the moment of the picking of the grapes. After harvesting, all rotten and less than ideal winemaking fruits for are separated from the ripe, superior grapes.

Crushing and pressing begins with the de-stemming of the selected grapes. In the past and for many years, humans would stomp on the grapes with their bare feet. Nowadays however, grapes are mechanically pressed and crushed, which is not only more hygienic, the method also prolongs the life of the wine. Mechanical pressing stomps grapes into must, which is just freshly pressed grape juice containing grape skin and seeds. To avoid undesirable colour and tannins from tarnishing white wine, the grape juice is separated from the skin and solids. In the world of wines, tannin is a textural element that gives wine its dry taste. It occurs naturally as a polyphenol in plants, fruit skins, seeds, leaves, bark, and wood. The skin remains during the production of red wine, as a measure to improve the taste, colour and tannins.

After pressing, the fermentation stage kicks in. Fermentation is a natural process during which sugar is broken down and converted into alcohol within 6 to 12 hours, aided very succinctly by the presence of wild yeast in the air. Dry wine is produced when all the sugar is broken down and converted. In the production of white wine, on the other hand, the fermentation process is interrupted to reserve of the sugar present in order to give it the sweet taste. Two types of fermentation are recognized: Hot fermentation is used for red wines, to increase colour and tannins; Cold fermentation is used for white and rosé wines and assist in the preservation of subtle aromas.

During the clarification process, the solids or such entities as tannins, proteins and dead yeast cells are separated from the wine. Wine is transferred into either oak barrel, which increases its exposure to oxygen, reducing tannins and adding fruity flavours; or steel tanks, which invigorates white wines and reduces exposure to oxygen, keeping the wine fresher. The wine is then clarified through either fining or filtration. During fining a substance, such as clay for example, will be included to the wine with the intention of attracting the unwanted particles, forcing it to drop to the bottom of the tank or barrel. Filtration involves filtering out any unwanted particles before placing the desired or filtered wine into another container for further aging or bottling.

Aging and bottling form part of the final procedure in the winemaking process. As explained, ageing is acquired either with oak or steel 'barrels. During bottling, the viticulturist has two options: cork or screwcap. Corks allow an indeterminate supply of oxygen into the mix, affecting how the wine tastes and permitting the wine to become 'corked'. Conversely, screwcaps control the amount of oxygen allowed to infiltrate the wine.

Wine Tasting & Drinking

We have all seen those people over the years, in fancy dining establishments and overlooking the lush lawns of up market wine estates, swirling and sniffing and sipping. But do we, or indeed they, really know what the seeming enigma of the somewhat ritual pre-drink dance is actually all about? Wine tasting is a rather precise art. Every little detail needs to be considered, even down to the environment in which one is wine-tasting, which may seem unimportant in the whole scheme of things but may affect the taste more than one cares to realise. Different smells or odours, a crowded or noisy room, a glass of the wrong size or shape - all can be to the detriment of achieving a clear sense of the wine's aromas. A reliable piece of advice: rinse the wine glass with the wine you'll be drinking rather than with water. This 'conditions' the glass and reduces the chances of the taste or aroma of the wine being marred.

One should evaluate the wine visually before drinking. This is best accomplished from all angles: straight angle view, side view, tilted view and eventually also swirling.

Why?

A straight angle view of the wine will give a sense of colour, which gives one a better understanding of the density and fullness of the wine.

A side view of the glass held in light will show the wine's clarity. A murky wine suggests one of two possibilities; either the wine has fermentation problems, or it is unfiltered or contains sediment due to being shaken.

A tilted view of the wine will help determine the age and weight; this is done by tilting the glass of wine towards the rim. A pale colour suggests the wine is thin and bland. A white wine with a brown appearance or a red wine appearing orange suggests the wine has become oxidised or is old.

The swirling of the wine will allow the formation of legs down the side of the wine glass. A wine with good tears or legs will indicate that it has a large content of alcohol.

Now that you have mastered the visual sensing, it is time for the sniffing. Start by swirling the glass, and one should hover the nose above the glass instead of burying it in the glass. Take a few short sniffs to detect the many different aromas and flaws in the wine. Aromas may be fruity, earthy, and that lent by the wine barrel. Flaws will present as a smell of burnt matches, old musty attic, vinegar, or nail polish. Fruity aromas are obvious due to the obvious fact that wine is made with grapes. Floral smells are less so (a good example of this would be from French wines), as are grassy or herbal scents. Earthy smells would include the scents of mushrooms, leather, damp earth and rock.

Clinking of glasses has been an important aspect of wine drinking since time immemorial. It is popularly believed that the early Europeans would clink their glasses to dispel evil spirits. Another supposition was that clinking provided the assurance that drinks were not poisoned by colliding the wine receptacles hard enough to spill the two drinks into each other. However, clinking of glasses during toasting came about long after poisoning was a threat or the popular belief that evil spirits lurked opportunistically in every corner. Toasting involves an announcement of blessings followed by drinking the alcohol. The term is believed to have been coined in a time in Britain when a communal container referred to as the loving cup was passed among revellers. Inside the cup was alcohol and a piece of bread, and it would do the rounds among the celebrants or guests, whereupon the host would consume the remaining alcohol along with the bread. Despite drinking from our own individual cup in modern times, we perpetuate the tradition of unity by clinking our glasses to maintain a communal connection to the announcement, or "toast" being made. Not only are the glasses making a connection during toasting, but also the people holding them. With toasting, all five senses are brought into the art of wine drinking. According to etiquette, one need not clink glasses with every individual in the crowd. If that was the case, stumbles would almost certainly cause wine spillage along the way. It is rather quite acceptable to simply make eye contact with those in the crowd when making a toast. The look will do the trick.

Tips on Choosing a Wine

A négociant is a wine merchant who amasses the produce of small growers and minor winemakers to sell under its own name. Négociants may purchase grapes, grape must, and wines in various phases of production.

How to order Wine in a Restaurant

The enjoyment of alcohol has escalated to become fairly pivotal in the restaurant dining experience. Pairing the wine with the food while perusing the restaurant menu affords diners a sensation of making an informed selection. Whether at a business dinner or lunch, or on a date, diners want to impress the table by selecting the right wine. This can be a stressful moment, especially when you're trying to make a good impression. Start off by discussing with the table whether they want a bottle to share or their own individual glass of wine and find out about their preferences. Secondly, set a price range. Next, if you're not confident choosing a wine, take advantage of the server or sommelier. Make sure to convey the necessary information in order to simplify the decision-making: red or white; fruity or earthy; light, medium or full-bodied and the price range. Once a decision has been made and the wine has been poured, you'll need to sample it by following the steps mentioned earlier on how to taste wine to make sure there are no flaws and that it fits all the diners at the table.

How to order wine like a sommelier

First of all, assess your particular environment. Is it classy or casual? If it's still early evening and you're starting the night, begin with a light and fruity wine which is easy to drink, resorting to the light and earthy wines, great for the slow drinkers. When seeking a crowd pleaser, bold and fruity is a sure winner. This will satisfy a crowd with various preferences. The next step it to size up the wine list: how is it organised? Pick a style of wine depending on the food or the mood, and then pick your price range. And finally, plan ahead. One bottle of wine will not suffice for a whole evening. The chances are you'll want to get richer and deeper wines as the evening progresses.

Champagne as a Wine

Let us first address the elephant in the room. Is there indeed a difference between Champagne and sparkling wine, or is it just geography with a hint of word play? The short answer is that all Champagne is sparkling wine, but not all sparkling wine is Champagne.

Which brings us to the differentiation. For Champagne to earn the title, it has to have been cultivated and produced in the French region of Champagne. By law in more than 70 countries, only this sparkling wine is allowed to bear the name Champagne. Grapes must be handpicked for the production of Champagne. Furthermore, these handpicked grapes must be pressed whole, in clusters, and then rest on the lees for at least 15 months. The finest quality cuvee Champagne could feasibly rest on the lees for as long as ten years. Only pinot noir, pinot meunier, and chardonnay grapes can be used to produce Champagne. Champagne has to be made in the Méthode Traditionelle, which entails the second fermentation process taking place in the same bottle from which it is served. The second fermentation process serves to return the resulting gas into the wine, for it to be freed once the cork is popped, as tiny bubbles.

Sparkling wine is frequently de-stemmed while it is resting on the lees. The chemistry behind producing Sparkling Wine is much the same as in the making of Champagne, only the technique for Sparkling wine is significantly shorter. Sparkling wine may be produced in mere months while Champagne may take up to a decade. The second fermentation process for Sparkling Wine takes place in pressurised tanks rather than in the bottle. It is the norm to use the Chenin blanc grape although the Sparkling Wine maker has carte blanche with that decision, to a point.

Back to Champagnes, since everyone has heard about the vintage Champagne, Dom Pérignon, it would be interesting to know a little about the person behind the name. Yes, Dom Pérignon was in fact a man of flesh and blood. By way of introduction, we must know first that the Benedictine Abbey at Hautvillers in France was thoroughly devastated during the French Wars of Religion. It was true to form rebuilt and its vineyards re-established such that by 1661 the Abbey boasted 25 acres, or ten hectares, of vineyards. As part of the tithes, the Abbey received grapes from the highly regarded vineyards of neighbouring Ay and Avenay-Val-d'Or. The Abbot progressed to having a cellar built and then looked to bringing on board a cellar master and treasurer to further the Abbey's bourgeoning winemaking industry. The man to fill the position in 1668 was none other than Pierre Perignon who was said to be quite the perfectionist. As such, he diligently improved the quality of the vineyards and its wines as well as the vinicultural practices of the Abbey. To him only

Pinot noir grapes were good enough to produce the best flavour and quality. The red grapes produced less bubbles than the more volatile whites did, and Pérignon considered the bubbles to be a fault that required attention to be diminished. Again, as it often is with wine, the rest is of course history.

There is a subtle trick to discerning between a Sparkling Wine and a Champagne. It is all in the bubbles, of course. Champagne has a refined effervescence with tiny bubbles. Sparkling Wine has a larger, more coarse fizz about it.

It is widely believed and contemplated as fact that Winston Churchill greatly enjoyed his Champagne. Indeed, Churchill did claim that the four essentials of life were: "Hot baths, cold champagne, new peas and old brandy." It is not disputed that Churchill drank some 42,000 bottles of Champagne, although over what term is debatable. The Champagne House of Pol Roger saw his as their ultimate brand ambassador, so much so that when he died the house famously edged the labels of its Brut NV with a distinct black border. In 1984 Pol Roger released the first 'Cuvée Sir Winston Churchill'.

How to open Champagne the right way

There is very much a right and a wrong way to open a bottle of Champagne. If you are going to be doing so publicly or with any form of audience whatsoever, your dignity would be best served by knowing the ins and outs of it, so to say. Even uncorking a bottle in private demands a level of knowledge so as not to unnecessarily waste any of the precious contents.

STEP 1: Rotate the tab to loosen the cage, just sufficient to breach the lip of the bottle. Do not remove it just yet but be careful to grip the cork and cage once it is no longer tightened.

STEP 2: Holding the bottle at a 45° angle, gently turn the base of the bottle all the while firmly keeping a hold of both the cork and the cage. This is a much safer alternative to attempts at turning the cage or the cork.

STEP 3: Apply pressure to the hold on the cage or cork when the sensation presents of the cork pushing out as a result of pressure from inside the bottle. Hold the bottle at the 45° angle for a second or so. To allow the pressure to escape without the champagne fountaining out of control.

Interesting Anecdotes

More than one story is credited with the accepted ritual in Formula 1 racing of the winner spraying champagne. This celebratory tradition is said to extend back to 1966 and happened quite by accident. The winner of the 1966 24-Hour Le Mans race, Joseph Siffert, inadvertently popped a less than adequately chilled bottle of champagne, showering the unwitting crowd of spectators.

Another version has the 1967 Le Man as venue, with Dan Gurney on the podium. Gurney had raced for Team Porsche and then made the decision to partner with Caroll Shelby to establish their own team, Anglo American Racers (AAR). Gurney unexpectedly won the 24 Hour-Le Mans race, affording the Ford team a victory in the overall standing for the second consecutive year. Ford Motor Company CEO Henry Ford II, team owner Caroll Shelby, and some journalists who had forecast a less than great race for their duet were gathered at the podium for the trophy ceremony. Gurney responded by shaking up the bottle of Moët and spraying the lot with champagne, apparently making *him* the one to start the tradition. His quote was, "What I did with the champagne was totally spontaneous. I had no idea it would start a tradition. I was beyond caring and just got caught up in the moment. It was one of those once-in-a-lifetime occasions where things turned out perfectly. I thought this hard-fought victory needed something special."

Wine by region

There are times when an old wine is just that. Old

The world is your oyster when it comes to gastronomic adventures and matters of symposiums, to coin an ancient term. However, much can be said about the variances in wines from different global regions. Wine is produced worldwide today. The basis for commercially viable wines is largely regional history and tradition, and regional and international economics. A sustainable venture within the given climate ultimately drives the economic reasoning, however. Climate must surely be a critical environmental aspect in producing a desirable wine. That being said, embodied in the notion of terroir are those complex influences that produce the unique traits of any wine. Terroir, from the Latin "territoire," basically encapsulates a stretch of land limited by its agricultural capacity, a concept traditionally embraced by the Cistercian monks in Burgundy, France back in the day.

France

France is famously renowned for its wines. Over the years, competition has increased as wines from certain wine regions around the world improve and muscle in on the originals. France boasts major wine growing regions numbering ten in total:

Alsace lies in the Rhine valley lower, along the eastern slopes of the Vosges mountains. Grapevines appeared hereabouts before man inhabited the area. Like Alsace itself, the wines produced here are unlike other wines and wine regions. This is thanks to Germanic traditions, since Alsace is on the German border. The region produces fruity or dry white wines primarily, with Sylvaner, Riesling, and the very fruity Gewurztraminer proving the most popular. The wines produced fall under a simple "Alsace" appellation, and the significant element will appear on each label, which is the grape variety; for example, Pinot. Alsace is not affected by the rules of 'Appellation control' applied throughout other wine growing regions of France.

Bordeaux is within Aquitaine which is of France's most famous three wine regions. Bordeaux dates back to 60 BC to the ancient Romans who were the first to cultivate and plant the vineyards and produce Bordeaux wine. In 1152, Eleanor of Aquitaine wed Henry ll, who would become England's king, thereby economically integrating the Aquitaine region into the Anglo-Norman world. The region of Bordeaux became the main wine supplier for England. Bordeaux wine exporting tradition aided the Bordeaux region to develop stronger commercial links in the centuries to follow. Wine exports to England began in 1302 from St. Emilion, with Saint Emilion being the first Bordeaux wine to be exported for King Edward l's pleasure. As one of the three big wine-producing areas of France, Bordeaux had the advantage of location, being that it lay along the Gironde river, which meets the Atlantic Ocean. It was therefore the only region directly accessing the ocean which afforded it the advantage as France's chief wine export region. There is no Bordeaux grape, so Bordeaux is comprised of a blend of red grapes: Cabernet Sauvignon and Merlot; and white grapes: Sémillon, Sauvignon blanc, Ugni blanc, Colombard, Merlot blanc. Full body, medium or full acidity, scents of black currant, plums, gravel, and lead are the characteristics that describe Bordeaux.

Burgundy vineyards lie within the narrow section of lad on the eastern slopes of the hills south east of Dijon. A good few million years ago, Burgundy was under the sea, and this created its limestone and marl soils, which are responsible for creating the sought-after minerality of Burgundian wines. The history of this region's wine dates back to around 50 BC when the Celts started producing wine before they were conquered by the Romans. They continued to produce wine in 'captivity', but after the falling of the Roman Empire the Catholic church took over the winemaking. This led to the Cistercian monks developing the art of Burgundian wines some two hundred years later. The Burgundy wine region produces the greatest and most requested red and white wines. It produces one hundred different appellations, from the largest which covers the entire Burgundy region, to the smaller appellations of the villages and vineyards. The idea behind the appellation system is the smaller and more precise the appellation, the better the quality. The main grapes grown around Burgundy are Pinot Noir and Chardonnay. Pinot Noir originated in Burgundy and makes up just a minimal portion of its overall wine production. Chardonnay is the primary grape for white wines and makes up almost half the wine production.

Champagne, also known worldwide as the bubbly that is cracked open for special celebratory occasions, originated in Champagne, in northern Europe. Champagne remains the only location in the world that produces Champagne. If the wine is not produced in Champagne, it is not considered to be Champagne. This winemaking region is not only unique but also boasts somewhat of a dramatic history in its chequered past. During the Medieval period, Champagne was the centre of European trade. During the Middle Ages the vineyards were run by the monks. The wine produced was blessed and used to celebrate the Eucharist, the Christian ceremony commemorating the Last Supper. On Christmas Day, 496 AD, the first king of France was baptised in Reims Cathedral and crowned king. The wine used to celebrate this special occasion was Champagne. As of 898, all the French kings were crowned in Reims (capital of Champagne) and Champagne would flow freely at the coronation banquets. Since the 19th Century, Champagne has been used at royal weddings and other special celebrations. Champagne is a White or Rosé sparkling wine, primarily fermented from the chardonnay, pinot noir, and pinot Meunier grapes. The sweetness level of Champagne ranges from Doux (up to 50 grams of sugar per litre) to Brut nature (no sugar, bone dry).

Rhône Valley is France's second largest wine region, producing predominantly red wine. Wines with a village name attached, indicate superiority. The wines produced in the Rhône Valley gain their unique flavour from the climate, soil, and the personal decisions of the wine maker at the time of the initial planting of the vineyards in the Rhône Valley. The Rhône Valley wine region is distinguished into two zones, Northern and Southern Rhône, both sharing the Rhône River as a border. The northern Rhône is cooled by severe cold north-westerly wind and has a continental climate. Syrah definitely dominates in this region, where White wines are produced from Marsanne, Viognier, and Roussanne. Major Syrah appellations are Crozes-Hermitage, Hermitage, Chateau-Grillet (Viognier), Cote-Rotie, Condrieu (Viognier), Saint-Joseph, and Saint-Peray, which produces white sparkling wines from Roussanne and Marsanne. With a milder climate moving effortlessly into the Mediterranean climate of Provence, southern Rhone is distinctly milder. The Red wines are produced from Cinsaut, Syrah, Grenache, Carignan, and Mourvedre, with the major appellations being Gigondas, Lirac, Chateauneuf du Pape, Tavel, Costieres de Nimes, and Vacqueyras. Tavel produces only Rosé wine. The whites are produced from Viognier, Roussanne, Marsanne, and Ugni Blanc. Dessert wines are made in the Rhone Valley, too, such as Condrieu, predominant in the north, and Muscat de Beaumes de Venise dominating the southern Rhone.

The Jura is located between Burgundy and Switzerland and enjoys a cool climate, clay and limestone soils and Jurassic era fossil matter, hence the name Jura. Jura is an ancient region going back to prehistoric times, but its wine industry is relatively new. Jura's two major styles of wine are vin jaune, which is yellow wine, and vin de paille, or straw wine, which taste like no other in the world. During the Middle Ages, locals discovered the Poulsard grape, from which a light but aromatic Red wine was produced. The grape was brought in from Burgundy which was known to have a lower quality product. Burgundy soon started producing Chardonnay and Pinot and Jura persistently produced good results with Poulsard. Poulsard's current dominance over Red wines remains accepted, but almost all the non-vin jaune are now made up of the Chardonnay which increased in popularity to make up White wine plantings. Before the vineyards were destroyed by the Phylloxera (tiny bug that eats the roots of European vines) disease in the 1800s, there were forty varieties of grapes. Only five remain: Ploussard, Pinot Noir, Trousseau, Chardonnay, and Savagnin. It's split into six regional appellations: Arbois, Côtes du Jura, L'Etoile, Crémant du Jura, Macvin du Jura and Château-Chalon.

Languedoc is situated on the Mediterranean Sea, with its grape vines originally brought over by the Greeks and Romans. Home to the Cathars, who believed that human life was trapped in a world created by a divinity identified with Satan, the robust region was more agony than pleasure for the religious sect that lived and worked the land. Alcohol, meat and material possessions were forbidden if one had any hope of joining God in heaven one day. Escaping Catholic oppression, the Cathars ended up in Spain, leaving behind their valuable land, ancient architecture, and a legacy as rich and storied as the wines now produced here. The vines of Languedoc were also destroyed by the Phylloxera. While Champagne, Burgundy, and Bordeaux were still recovering, Languedoc made a rapid revival and was able to supply the whole of France with wine. In the 1980s, wine farmers began expanding their range by growing Pinot Noir, Sauvignon Blanc, Cabernet, Merlot and Chardonnay. The typical Languedoc Red is a medium-bodied, fruity wine. Examples of the finest red wines have darker, more savoury aromas and hints of undergrowth, spice and leather, and are slightly heavier-bodied. Classic southern French varieties of grape such as Syrah, Grenache, and Mourvèdre, with a hint of Cinsaut or Carignan are used to make these.

Lorraine is a small wine producing area in north east France, slightly west of Alsace. Today the area barely shows up on our radar as a wine producer, but once upon a time vines flourished here. Before Appellation "crontrôlée" regulations, a large quantity of the grapes for Champagne were sourced from this area. Phylloxera arrived here much later than in Champagne, which meant that the grapes harvested from this source were of immense benefit to the industry. After 1871 Lorraine became a part of the German Empire, until 1918. Today three stages of production are accepted, with a clear connection between them with the same grapes traditionally being grown: Auxerrois, Elbling, Gamay, Müller-Thurgau (Rivaner), Pinot Blanc, Pinot Gris, Pinot Noir and some Gewurztraminer.

Loire Valley produces excellent wines featuring only very few Loire wines, Rosés, Whites, or pale Reds amongst the finest French wines. Loire valley must be the second largest producer of sparkling wines, after Champagne, in France. Touraine is known for light Red wines, particularly made with the Gamay grape. Vin gris (grey wine), a very pale Rosé, and a White wine made from black grapes are almost made here.

Provence is France's 'primogenital' wine producing region. Its origins can be tracked back 26 centuries when Phoenicians planted vines in 600 BC. The region wasn't known for producing particularly good wine, and only recently has Provence started to produce wines resulting in the area's popularity among wine connoisseurs. The name Provence was given to the region by the Romans when they settled there four centuries after the Phoenicians. As the Roman Empire conquered the surrounding areas and extended its borders, wine production increased considerably. After the Empire fell, the vines were no longer developed. By 100 BC, the wine makers introduced the process of short soaking before the fermentation process, producing wines of a pale, rose-petal colour. This pale wine, known today as Rosé, became well-known as the prestigious drink of aristocrats. Provence produces more Rosé than any other wine. Rosé is made from red grapes and winemakers reduce the grape skin contact to avoid darker juice pigmentation. The grapes are pressed immediately after picking to hold both the freshness and the pale hue. The complex aromas and flavours develop by blending small-batch, single-variety Rosés, and then combining them into a final blend in stainless-steel tanks or oak barrels. Blending varieties include Grenache, Rolle, Syrah, Mourvèdre, Carignan, Cinsault, Counoise, Cabernet Sauvignon, and Tibouren.

South-west is called France's Hidden Corner, nestled as it is with Spain and the Pyrénées Mountains to the south, the Atlantic Ocean on the west, and Bordeaux to the north. Each wine producing region here abouts has village and communal appellations also known as Appellation d'Origine Protégée (protected designation of origin), meaning these appellations must obey strict regulations on growing grapes and wine production. Bergerac & Dordogne River, located south of Bordeaux with the vineyards lying along the Dordogne River, produce Bordeaux, Cabernet Sauvignon, and Merlot. As far as grapes go, you'll find the same varieties as in Bergerac & Dordogne, with a few additions to boot. Lot River is the origin of Malbec and is influenced by both the Atlantic and the Mediterranean climates and grows the same grape varieties as the Garonne & Tarn. Cahors is a famous sub-region for producing Malbec revered for centuries by the royal houses of Russia and England. Pyrénées produces rare rustic and artisanal wines, produced from the local Tannat grape.

Italy

Italy's diverse wine history dates back more than two thousand years. Italy produces a remarkable amount of wine each year, the biggest being in 2012 when they produced a remarkable 4 billion litres. Their rivals in wine production are France and Spain, which both produce significant volumes each year. There are 20 wine regions in Italy, the main 6 being Veneto, Tuscany, Piedmont, Sicily, Emilia-Romagna, and Lombardy.

We'll start off with the most productive wine region of Italy; Veneto, located in North-eastern Italy. The region produces more wine than the rest of the country, despite being of the smallest areas. Its most celebrated appellations are Prosecco, the sparkling wine produced from the Glera grape. Prosecco has become an inexpensive substitute for Champagne.

The picturesque **Tuscany** houses Italy's most scenic vineyards and is its most ancient wine-producing region, going all the way to the 8th Century BC. Tuscany's wines are based firmly on the Sangiovese grape, bottled as Chianti, which are incorporated into Italy's blended wines. Sangiovese produces acidic, tannic wines in a range of flavours, from fruity to earthy. Tuscany's supreme White must be Vernaccia di San Gimignano, which is produced from the Vernaccia grape with its resultant crisp and citrusy flavour.

Piedmont, nestled in the Po River Valley, borders the frosty Alps of the north and is the source of Italy's celebrated Reds, produced from Nebbiolo grapes: Barolo ("King of Wines") progresses a rich fragrance with traces of truffle, liquorice, and rose, and is well paired with red meats; Barbaresco. And because it is close to the Mediterranean, the fog assists with the ripening of the Nebbiolo grape. Popular grapes produced in Piemonte, are Dolcetto and Barbera, both considered more everyday wines with soft tannins that are best imbibed young.

Sicily, the largest of the Mediterranean islands, has perfect wine growing conditions and is home to the most of Italy's vineyards. The more renowned wine hereabouts is the sweet Marsala, which is a wine fortified with brandy that is enjoyed as a sipping wine and often used in cooking. Zibibbo is a sweet wine resultant from allowing the grapes to ferment in the sun, leaving it with a reduced alcohol content. Nero d'Avola is a rich, full-bodied red wine with high acidity and vigorous tannins.

Emilia-Romagna, one of the country's oldest wine producing areas, is a large and fertile region which encapsulates almost all of central Italy from the east to the west coast. The well-known **Lambrusco**, a sparkling red wine produced from the Lambrusco grape was first cultivated by the ancient Etruscans and dominates here. Lambrusco pairs extremely well with creamy lasagne and goes onto improving digestion. Varieties also produced in the region include Sangiovese, Malvasia, Barbera and Trebbiano.

Lombardy is among the largest Italian wine regions, surrounded by many lakes, one being Lake Garda, which helps moderate the temperate around the vineyards that are located in northern Italy. Lombardy, however, has only two wine styles: Franciacorta and Valtellina. Vines have been cultivated around the shores of Lake Garda for centuries. The climate-moderating effect of each of these lakes is particularly valuable in the cooler, more elevated areas. Franciacorta DOCG is the best known of the sparkling wines, and can only be produced hereabouts, produced from grapes grown on the slopes of Lake Iseo. Chardonnay, Pinot Nero and Pinot Bianco are permitted, and the best examples have much in common with Champagne. Only wines from the best vineyards are eligible for the DOCG, which is for sparkling wines only. Valtellina is the most respected area for red wine production and its wines are especially popular with the Swiss, particularly those wines made with Nebbiolo. Valtellina can only be produced in this region, like the Franciacorta, and must be comprised 90% of Nebbiolo grapes.

Spain

Viticulture has been a part of Spain since before the Phoenicians founded the Cadiz trading post around 100 BC. There's evidence to prove that vineyards were planted in the Peninsula 65 million to 2.6 million years ago. The Carthaginians improved the wine making techniques of the Phoenicians when they arrived in the Peninsula. But the real wine history and culture began after the Romans won the Punic Wars against the Carthaginians and the Peninsula became part of the Roman Empire, who named it Hispania. Rioja makes up the heart of red wines in Spain, produced from the Tempranillo grape. Viura is its dominant white grape with white wines comprising a mere 10% of the region's wine production. Rioja has three unique districts: Rioja, Alta and Rioja Alavesa are cooler while Rioja Baja is balmier. The Spanish wine bottle labels are:

Crianza, a fresh, fruity and youthful red, aged in oak for at least one year followed by a year aging in the bottle;

Reserva is produced from the Tempranillo grape with its impressive cherry flavours. Reserva must age for at least one year in the barrel and another two years in either the barrel or the bottle;

Gran Reserva require barrel aging for two years followed by another three years in the bottle.

Rioja is Spain's most famous wine region. Varying in style, it usually produces earthy and fruity flavours, with a smooth taste. The mixture of grapes from this region often combines sweet flavours with sour and rich, producing some of the most unique wines.

Penedès is one of the best and oldest of the Spanish wine regions, set amongst the coastal hills of Catalonia. Cava, a sparkling white wine which is competition to Champagne and Prosecco, is among the region's most famous and the best of European sparkling wines. Mostly white grapes are grown here, but the few red grapes produce particularly excellent red wines. These Reds are left to age in oak barrels.

Priorat is famous for its vineyards growing precariously on dangerously steep terraces along hills and mountains. These vines must dig extra deep to find water and nutrients in the slate soil of Priorat.

Ribera del Duero is located on the high plateau in Burgos province. It has dry, hot summers followed by harsh, cold winters and minimal rainfall. The grapes are almost all red, with the only white grape being the Albillo.

The **Valencia** wine region has grown grapes since the Neolithic era in the sandy, chalky, limestone-rich soil. Its wine is exported all around the world. Moscato grapes are grown here. Crianza wines are cask-aged for only three months, in comparison to Reserva wines which are aged for a very minimum of six months.

Navarra region produces Rosado (Rosé) and Red wines, which makes up 95% of its wine production.

La Mancha has more than 22 000 grape-growers and three hundred wineries. It is known for producing delicious Tempranillo and Garnacha wines.

Rueda is in Castilla y Leon. Its crisp White wines are produced from the Verdejo grape. Bodegas Menade Rueda Verdejoi combines mineral and nutty, and creamy and dry, to produce a fresh wine with body.

Jumilla wine region takes up a great deal of Murcia and boasts some 3,000 grape-growers over 32 000 hectares.

Jerez/Sherry gained its popularity because of its coastal location and resultant prosperity in overseas exploration and trade. Some of the greatest wines produced here are hand-produced and can be described as almondy, dry, crisp and light.

United States

Wild grapes grew in abundance in the early days of Napa Valley, but it took settler George Calvert Yount to discover the area's potential for cultivating wine grapes. He was the first to plant Napa Valley grapes in 1839. Soon after, other pioneers helped introduce the first vitis vinifera grapes to the area. Charles Krug is credited with establishing Napa Valley's first commercial winery in 1861 and his success sparked a wave of new growth. By 1889 the are boasted more than 140 wineries. Today, Napa Valley is among the world's leading wine-making regions. It's manicured vineyards, impressive Chardonnays, world-famous Cabernet Sauvignons, velvety Merlots, sparkling wines, light Sauvignon Blanc, silky Pinot Noir, and bold Zinfandel are world renowned.

Sonoma, California, often termed Napa's more rustic and relaxed sibling, was America's First Wine Country. In 1821, Russian colonists planted and cultivated grapes on the Pacific coast, but it was the Spanish Franciscan fathers who laid the foundation for the wine production way back in 1832 when they planted several thousand grapevines in Sonoma. In 1834, political upheaval brought an appropriation of the missions by the Mexican government. During this period of disarray, cuttings from the Sonoma Mission vineyards were carried throughout the northern California area to start new vineyards. This wine region is now home to award winning wines and 17 distinct appellations. They are famous for their Cabernet Sauvignons, Pinot Noirs, and Chardonnays.

Willamette Valley, Oregon, lies on the same latitude as the France's Burgundy region. Since Burgundy is renowned for its Pinot Noir, it comes as little surprise that Pinot Noir also fairs well here. The fertile Willamette Valley was not surprisingly popular when pioneers first started to settle in the old West in the early 19th Century. It was however only in the 1960s that Viticulture really took root. Thanks go to the University of California's Davis campus whose students first looked north for inspiration when then Californian climate proved unsuitable for Pinot Noir. The rest is so to say history.

Charlottesville, Virginia is where Thomas Jefferson nearly 250 years ago first cultivated grapes at his home, Monticello. He may not have reaped much success, but the lengthy growing season, rustic landscape, and fertile soil, have produced several award-winning wines since then.

Hill Country is the Texan Vinicultural region, over nine million acres. Its dry, sunny climate produces fine Albarinos, Cabernets, Tempranillos, Syrahs, and Zinfandels.

Finger Lakes, New York produces Gewürztraminer and Chardonnay. The areas boasts some 120 wineries, known for their cool climate wines. These wines are from grapes that are suited to withstand the typical long, cold winters. The top variety is Riesling, a vinifera (classic European) grape that produces sweet and dry wines.

Paso Robles, California, lies between Los Angeles and San Francisco, and is possibly most known for its Cabernet Sauvignon. Its unexpected, hidden ems besides these include the excellent white Rhône-style blends, Merlot, Zinfandel, and Syrah.

Argentina

Argentina's wine story began way back in the 16th century with the transporting of vines from Spain, thanks to the conquistadors and Spanish missionaries. Much wine came from these vines, but the produce was not great. Criolla was by far the most popular of the varietals, but it produced a somewhat crude wine. It did however form the basis of the wine production ad industry in the country. Argentina took a leaf out of their neighbour, Chile's, book and upped their game to produce export quality wines for the American and European markets.

Over the past decade Argentina has evolved from a country unknown on the global wine scene to the fastest growing exporter of wines in the New world. The foremost grape in terms of quantity and reputation is Malbec. This Bordeaux variety was imported from France in the 1800s. Cabernet Sauvignon, Bonarda, Syrah, Tempranillo Merlot, and Pinot Noir are among the Reds produced. White wines are Pinot Grigio, Chardonnay, and Sauvignon Blanc. Their signature grape, however, produces a floral, tropical-tasting wine and is known as Torrontés. The three wine sub-regions of

Argentina are as follows:

Cuyo is the largest and most productive region, the heart of Malbec country, and known for excellent examples of the Italian grape Bonarda.

Patgonia, lying south of Argentina, grows many cooler-climate wines such as Pinot Noir, Gewürztraminer and Riesling.

Catamarca, Juju and Salta are part of the region referred to as the North-West. These are known as among the highest altitude vineyards.

South Africa

South Africa's wine industry has been largely underestimated for much of the 20th Century, due mostly to politics. Economic and political isolation resulted from boycotts of South African products during the height of the country's Apartheid era. When the Apartheid government was replaced, and bans were lifted, the world began rediscovering South Africa.

The South African wine industry goes back to the 17th century in Constantia, a suburb of Cape Town. The vineyards in this area are considered to produce some of the greatest wines in the world, and still produce wine today. South African wine production can be traced to the Dutch East India Company when Cape Town was a station along the spice route. Vineyards were planted to produce fruits, juices, and wine to supplement the passing seamen and prevent scurvy in the ships' sailors. By the early 1900's, over 80 million vines were planted. In 1918, the government of the day formed the KWV (Koöperatieve Winjnbouwers Vereniging van Zuid-Afrika Bpkt). In 1973, it created South Africa's version of the French AOC (Appellation d'Origine) termed the WO (Wine of Origin). There are nine wine regions throughout South Africa:

Constantia is a historical region with its vineyards tucked away on Constantia Mountain. On the slopes they are cooled by Cape town's sea breezes. In the 18th and 19th Centuries, the area was famed for its legendary dessert wine, Vin de Constance. Nowadays, Constantia is more known for its Bordeaux Blend wines, Sauvignon Blanc and dessert wines produced from Muscat Blanc. The Constantia estate originated in 1685, laid by Simon van der Stel, the second Governor of the Cape of **Good** Hope.

Elgin is a newish, cool-climate region east of Stellenbosch, which is still predominantly a fruit-growing area.

Franschoek is situated in a valley and is a small but noteworthy region, inland of Stellenbosch. Its relatively high rainfall and variety of soils allows for the production of many wine styles.

Paarl is a well-known region north-west of Cape Town, where the Western Cape's best-known wineries are located. Its Mediterranean climate has resulted in its focus moved more to the reds from being a traditionally White wine region, Shiraz Cabernet Sauvignon, Chenin Blanc, Pinotage, and Chardonnay are all important grape varieties in the region. Paarl's huge variation of terroir (soil, landscape, climate) affords wine farmers vast opportunities to experiment with many grape varieties and blends. The red wines are rich and full-bodied, with a great intensity of fruit. The white wines are fruit driven and tropical.

Robertson is next to Worcester and is rather illogically best known for its White wines. Graham Beck, De Wetshof, and Springfield are some of the leading wine producers of this region which also boasts a good many brandy refineries.

Stellenbosch is the South Africa's most famous wine producing area, lying inland from Cape Town, it houses many leading wine estates. The granite-based soils are perfected suited for producing fine red wines, while the sandstone soils are best for White wines. Stellenbosch produces Cabernet Sauvignon, Sauvignon Blanc, Shiraz and Chenin Blanc. Stellenbosch is also famous for being the birthplace of Pinotage as recently as 1924.

Swartland is traditionally a wheat-producing region, and is now focusing on making rich, fruit-driven wines mainly from the Shiraz, Chenin Blanc and Pinotage grape varieties.

Walker Bay is respected for the Burgundian-styled Pinot Noir and Chardonnay that they produce, as well as Sauvignon Blanc.

The vineyards of **Worcester** are protected from extreme weather by mountain ranges on every side and produce about a quarter of all the country's wine. The region produces a wide variety, offering Chenin Blanc, Sauvignon Blanc and Colombard. Shiraz, Pinotage and with Cabernet Sauvignon among the principal red wine grape varieties.

Chile

Chile's wine legacy started when Spanish monks brought wine grapes to the country way back in 1548. The vine bearing monks soon discovered that the soil and climate were perfect for producing great grapes. By the time Chile declared its independence from Spain in 1810, it had a flourishing wine industry. The Denomination of Origin system (D.O.) demarcates four large winegrowing regions:

Coquimbo is divided into three smaller regions. Elqui produces fruit and wines; Limari suffers with little rainfall; and Choapa has no wineries, only vineyards.

Aconcagua gets water for the vineyards off the snow-covered mountains of the same name. Casablanca is a newer wine sub-region in Chile and was only planted after the revival of the wine industry in the 1980s.

Central Valley is the most famous wine region in Chile. Maipo's Cabernet Sauvignons are well-regarded,

Southern Regions has three sub-regions: Itata grows Moscatel de alejandría. The same goes for Bío, although state-of-the-art growers introduced non-traditional varieties of wine grapes, such as Gewürtztraminer and Pinot noir. While Malleco producers produce Chardonnays and Pinot noirs.

China

Grape wine is the type preferred in the Western countries and archaeological evidence shows that grape wine in China originated about 4 600 years ago, earlier than the known history of rice wine. However, Yellow Liquor (Huang Jiu) and White Liquor (Bai Jiu) have taken over the Chinese wine culture for thousands of years. Remains on pottery fragments found in the Neolithic site of Jiahu are recognised as coming from a fermented beverage containing honey, rice, and fruit, dating to 7000–6600 BC.

Shandong Peninsula and Hebei Province on the monsoonal east coast, produce more than half China's wine production. Cabernet Gernischt, is the most widely grown grape type here.

The Yunnan plateau has a long growing season and a humid climate. Lying below the ideal zone for wine growing, near the Tibet border, it is cooled by heights of up to 2500 meters.

Ningxia and Shanxi are well known for their high-quality wine.

Xinjiang province sees dramatic temperatures fluctuations between day and night, and rainfall is often bordering on drought levels. Grapes reach high sugar and low acidity levels. Viticulture is a fast-growing industry here, with production focusing more on sweet wines.

Surprising Wine regions

Wine has an interesting and chequered past. With its roots in piety and religion, its vines have reached ever more adventurously into new and unexpected parts of the world, far removed from the well-known and expected sources of the ambrosia of the gods. While technology and adventure have accounted for some of the newer grapes making themselves known recently, some areas have unearthed their long secret historic links to viticulture.

Lebanon

Wine production began here at least 5 000 years ago. It was in this region of Canaan that Jesus changed water into wine at the wedding of Cana. The term 'wine' comes from a Phoenician word describing the fermentation of grapes. Even though the Phoenicians did not invent wine, they perfected the cultivation of grapevines and used it as a source of income. As a matter of interest, the underwater explorer who discovered the Titanic wreck, Robert Ballard, also discovered Phoenician ships dating back to 750 BC, which had been carrying a cargo of wine that remained unharmed Phoenicians stored wine in an ancient Greek jar with two handles and a narrow neck, called an amphora. To stop oxidation they layered the amphora with olive oil and sealed it with pine and resin. The Egyptians could not produce as good quality a wine as the Phoenician's, and therefore were soon major consumer of their wines. The Greeks learned the art from the Phoenicians and then spread the knowledge through Europe.

The most common red grape varieties are Cinsaut, Carignan, Cabernet Sauvignon, Merlot and Syrah and prominent white varieties are Chardonnay, Sauvignon Blanc and Clairette. The high-quality red wines from Bekaa Valley have strong similarities to the Bordeaux wines.

Bekaa Valley is Lebanon's main wine-growing region and could very well be the birthplace of wine. This is where the modern wines of Lebanon are developed, with about 90% of the country's wine produced here. The vineyards inside Bekaa Valley are on a plateau lying at an altitude of 1 000 meters. They have ideal conditions including warm summers, cool nights and low rainfall. The plateau is protected against winds by the surrounding mountains which also bring water to the vineyards.

Georgia

Wine has been produced here for thousands of years, which make this of the oldest wine-producing countries in the world, with many native grape varieties eventually used for wine making. Archaeological findings that are 9 000 years old indicate ancient wine production. In fact, the Georgian word "ghvino" may well be the root of "vin," "vino," and eventually, "wine."

Ikhalto became important in grapevine cultivation. Georgia was a largely Christian nation, left at peace during the surrounding battles.

During the Ottoman occupation most of this region was plunged into prohibition because of Muslim law. Georgia continued its wine production because the rules made allowances for Christian ceremonial wines.

Georgian wines thrived until the Phylloxera epidemic affected them and brought suffering for some decades. Wine is still produced throughout the republic despite marketing problems. The country has five vinicultural zones: Racha-Lechkumi, Kakheti, Imereti, Kartli, and the Black Sea Coast.

Japan

Grapes were almost only consumed as a fresh fruit for hundreds of years, and that they could be dried or fermented took off in the mid-1800s during the Meiji Restoration. Grape growers saw differences between wine grapes and table grapes. Foreign grapes led to 61 varieties of table grapes and 28 varieties of wine grapes.

Hokkaido, an island situated north of Japan, is Japan's coldest and second largest island. The volcanic plateaus and mountains that make up the geography of the island result in relatively cool summers and snowy or icy winters, which make vineyard management somewhat tricky. Vines are buried underground in autumn to protect the delicate flower buds on the vines against freezing. A few well-known wine brands in Hokkaido are Hokkaido Wine Company and Tokachi Wine.

The first varieties planted in the region were Pinot Blanc, Muller-Thurgau and Zweigelt. Now Chardonnay, Pinot Noir, Merlot and Kerner are widely grown here.

Yamagata is situated between Hokkaido and Yamanashi. The region experiences high humidity and a little sunshine daily, which creates an ideal environment for powdery mildew and bunch rot. Since this region suffers frequent typhoons during many months of the year, it has become a matter of survival of the fittest within the grapevine 'society'.

Yamanashi, known as the "Kingdom of Fruit", is located in the Chūbu region. Grapevines in this region normally have very deep roots due to the water runoff from surrounding mountains. With over 80 wineries, this region is accountable for about 40% of Japan's wine production. The Japanese wine industry originated in Katsunuma. The grape variety Koshu is the most widely planted variety in Yamanashi and is a cross between a light Pinot Grigio and Semillon.

Nagano has a humid subtropical climate, which makes it a challenging area in which to grow vines. Hot and humid summers are followed by cold and snowy winters which are both topped off with the occasional typhoon. The regions produces fresh, herbaceous, intense, light, and highly drinkable wines that truly capture the region's characteristics. Wineries in this area produce multiple grape varieties including Chardonnay, Merlot and Muscat Bailey A grapes.

New Zealand

Samuel Marsden, an Anglican minister, was the first to plant grapevines at the Bay of Islands in 1819. The earliest winemaker was the Scotsman, James Busby, the first selected British Resident in New Zealand. Grape Varieties grown in New Zealand are Sauvignon Blanc, Pinot Noir, Chardonnay, Pinot Gris, Cabernet Sauvignon, Merlot, Syrah, Riesling, Gewurztraminer, Viognier, Malbec, Tempranillo, Marzemino, Semillon. There are 12 wine regions in New Zealand:

Marlborough put New Zealand on the international wine map Blanc in the 1980s with the very good Sauvignon. Marlborough accounts for over 20,000 hectares of vineyards, making it the country's largest wine growing region. Marlborough wineries offer a huge range of varieties, from Pinot Noir to Chardonnay.

Hawke's Bay has earned itself a highly recognised reputation for producing high quality Cabernet and Merlot blends, Syrah, Chardonnay, Pinot Noir and a remarkable selection of aromatic white wines. Grape vines were first planted in the Hawke's Bay in 1851. The warm climate and lengthy growing season allow for the successful production of dessert wines.

Central Otago is famous for producing great aromatics, Chardonnay and Sauvignon Blanc and flourishing Pinot Noir.

Gisborne is home to a mix of large producers, boutique wineries, and commercial growers who are continuously exploring new varieties and vineyard sites. Chardonnay is the dominant variety with Pinot Gris being the second largest wine variety. Rich in history, Gisborne claims Captain Cook's first landfall, as well as being the first place in New Zealand to see the sunrise.

The **Canterbury** wine region covers 200km of the eastern coastline of the South Island. Pinot Noir, Chardonnay and aromatics take prime position here with a cool, dry climate and a long growing season that encourages varietal expression of note. Canterbury Plains first say vineyards established in 1978. Soon after North Canterbury and regions south-west of Christchurch were also cultivated. Vines are now planted from Cheviot in the north to Waimate in the south.

Wairarapa, a boutique region, has a range of styles and varieties on offer, such as Pinot Noir, Sauvignon Blanc and aromatics, as well as

Chardonnay, Syrah and dessert wines. The three main sub-regions in the area are Martinborough, Gladstone and Masterton. While they share a similar soil structure and climate, each offer delicate differences on the palate.

Nelson is a boutique wine region producing outstanding Pinot Noir, Chardonnay, Sauvignon Blanc and aromatics, and an impressive mix of developing varieties. Long famous for its generous crops and orchards, Nelson's wine roots were cultivated in the mid-1800s, when German settlers planted the area's first grape vines which went on to produce wine. Pioneering 1970s producers established the modern wine industry, with iconic names such as Seifried and Neudorf still going strong.

Auckland is home to some of New Zealand's largest wine companies, as well as high-quality, boutique wineries. The local sub-regions are united by volcanic, clay-rich soils, and a mild sea climate. Waiheke Island in the Hauraki Gulf is home to Syrah, world-class Chardonnay, Cabernet blends and fine aromatics. West Auckland is renowned for its internationally recognised, elegant Chardonnay and stylish Merlot. To the North of Auckland, excellent Cabernet blends, Pinot Gris and Syrah are produced, with numerous emerging red varieties being vinified with great success.

Northland's Chardonnays, Pinot Gris and vibrant Viogniers are leading the white wine growth. Red wines produced include spicy Syrahs, stylish Cabernet and Merlot blends, peppery Pinotages and complex Chambourcin. Extending from Karikari in the north to Mangawhai in the south, each vineyard in Northland is unique in aspect, soil, and micro-climate.

Waitaki Valley, in North Otago, enjoys hot, dry summers, cold winters and long dry autumns. These climatic characteristics overlay the complex geology of the Waitakian Limestones and wines of distinction result and reflect the origin. Their signature varieties include Pinot Noir, Pinot Gris, Riesling, Chardonnay and Gewurztraminer. These wines are distinguished by their terroir and are rapidly growing a reputation for their quality and uniqueness.

Waikato Wine styles are focused mainly on Pinot Noir, Pinot Gris, with Sauvignon Blanc occupying third place.

Bay of Plenty Wine production is focused mainly on Pinot Noir, Pinot Gris, with Sauvignon Blanc occupying third place.

India

Grape growing and viticulture has been traced to the Bronze Age, when Persian traders introduced it to the India. Wine made from grapes or fermented grain drinks became commonplace in the greater regions. Phylloxera hit at the start of the 20th century, and very nearly wrecked the industry. Wine production only made its return in the 1980s. This return coincided most coincidentally with the growing middle class which was taking more of an interest in dining out and luxury goods. Seventy Indian wine producers produce 24 million bottles per year. The main red grapes are Cabernet Sauvignon, Merlot, Shiraz, and Pinot Noir. White varieties include Chenin Blanc, Sauvignon Blanc, and Chardonnay. Two main winegrowing regions are Nashik near Mumbai, in the state of Maharashtra, and Nandi Hills near Bangalore in Karnataka.

Nashik is home to 29 wineries and advertised as India's wine capital. Kanwal Grover experimented with grape varieties during the 1970s and invested in vineyards. Grover Zampa vineyard is among India's finest wineries now and produces Bordeaux-style and Cabernet Sauvignon blends under a French wine consultant's supervision.

Most of the wine produced in Morocco is Red. Small quantities of White wine are produced from Chenin Blanc, French classics Muscat and Clairette, Sauvignon Blanc and Chardonnay.

Morocco

Morocco has the best natural potential for producing quality wines due to its location. High mountains and the cooling Atlantic balance the risk of the vineyards getting too hot. Morocco exported wine in the colonial era before 1956, and their wine industry is currently making a comeback, with marked expansion due to the influx of foreign investment since the 1990s.

Viticulture in this region was introduced by Phoenician settlers and established in the time of Ancient Rome. At the time of the country's independence in 1956, there was 55 000 hectares (140,000 acres) under cultivation for wine making. After Morocco gained independence from France many of the French wine experts left Morocco. Competition from overproduction in other Mediterranean countries combined with restricted access to the traditional market saw much of the wine making becoming unproductive. Many of the country's vineyards were replaced with other crops.

Carignan, Cinsaut, Grenache, Syrah, Cabernet Sauvignon and Merlot are their red varieties that are currently growing, which are more popular than their white varieties; Chenin Blanc, southern French classics Muscat, Clairette, Sauvignon Blanc and Chardonnay.

Ethiopia

Looking at the wine making heritage in Ethiopia is pretty much as old as Ethiopia as a country. Grapes date back to this region as far the early Axumite time around the time of the first century A.D when wine would most certainly have been imported through the Red Sea Port of Adulis. Carvings in the great standing obelisk at Axum dating to 200 A.D. further evidence Axumite knowledge of grapes and wines. Reference to Axumite wine appears in early 4th century inscriptions. Ethiopian produced wines include Cabernet Sauvignon, Syrah, Merlot, and Chardonnay.

Polynesia

The country has only one wine label, Vin de Tahiti. Dominique Auroy, the wine enthusiast and wealthy French businessman, planted the seed to create a winery in French Polynesia, and vines were first imported in 1992from France and Italy. The extensive preliminary works managed by Dominique included shipping in 200 tons of Tahiti earth to ensure the vines would establish to their best ability. Being unsure where best to cultivate, acclimatization tests were carried out by planting vineyards throughout its five groups of islands. Going by the results, seven acres were laid on a small coral island in Rangiroa in 1997. The country's first harvests were made in 1999 and 2000, and by 2003, 800 bottles were produced by the winery per year. The vineyard now produces more 40 000 bottles per year, cultivate over 8 hectares.

The terroir of the vineyard here is unique since the ground is primarily coral and the soil is improved by natural compost made from algae. Sea spray is harmful to grapes, and so its location became a problem, requiring irrigation despite the vineyards being surrounded by water. A well was sunk at the lowest point such that the water table was accessed, and this natural source of ground water is utilized through a drip irrigation system. Since the region experiences no cold season, it became vital to fool the vines into believing winter temperatures were in fact in place. Pruning brings about stress that causes the blooming of new buds, kickstarting the life cycle. These grapes are harvested twice a year to normal harvesting once a year. May and December therefore become their austral winter and austral summer harvests.

Austria

Austria has enjoyed a revival as a wine-producer. Its slightly warmer climate compared to Germany shows in the wine styles. The focus is largely on Red wines while retaining their classics, such as sweet Ausbruch and Strohwein. It is simultaneously developing modern wines, including the signature white, crisp, aromatic Gruner Veltliner. 35 grape varieties are officially allowed in Austrian quality wine, of which almost two-thirds are white-wine varieties. These are Blanc, Welschrieslin, Sauvignon, Chardonnay, and Pinot Blanc, known as Weissburgunder. Austria's red wines are made primarily from Saint-Laurent, Zweigelt, Blaufrankisch, and Pinot Noir (Blauburgunder). Gruner Veltliner is by far the most important, followed by Riesling.

Vine cultivation in Austria goes back to Roman times. Evidence of this suggests that vines were planted here 2 000 years ago.

Australia

Australia has no native grape vines. To produce local wine, grapevines were first imported in 1788, with cuttings arriving aboard a ship from the Cape of Good Hope. The first vines were cultivated in Sydney at Farm Cove. The intense heat and humidity resulted in the vines rotting. John Macarthur was the aspiring viticulturist who planted vines in the early in the 1800s, and it is he who is to thank for the first winery and commercial vineyard.

In 1833, James Busby introduced the now-famous Syrah or Shiraz to the country, bringing cuttings from Spain and France. European grapes have had some success here, including Merlot, Chardonnay, and Grenache. With so many European varietals, phylloxera affected the region hard when it hit in 1875, and most of the vines were lost to the bug. When it became evident that American vines were more capable of resisting phylloxera, vintners Franken-vined their grapevines by grafting European vines to American plants. European grapes were in this way grown on plants with pest-resistant roots.

Australia has three major wine regions, namely South Australia, New South Wales and Victoria.

South Australia makes up about 50% of Australia's wine production. Many vineyards in South Australia produce cheap wines for their home market, but vineyards closer to Adelaide make the country's finest wines. Adelaide's finest vineyards are in:

Barossa Valley, among Australia's oldest wine producing areas which produces fine wines. This region is famous for its full-bodied Cabernet Sauvignon, Shiraz, and Grenache, and Semillon and Riesling.

Clare Valley produces the best dry and crisp style Rieslings, and a fine Shiraz and Cabernet Sauvignon.

McLaren Vale has a mild climate influenced by the sea and is mainly well-regarded for its Shiraz, Cabernet, Sauvignon Blanc, and Chardonnay.

Adelaide Hills is a fairly cool region that sits between the Barossa and McLaren Vale areas and produces Chardonnay, Sauvignon Blanc, Pinot Noir, and Shiraz.

Limestone Coast is an important area for both red and white fine wines, because of the presence of limestone in the soil. Its known as the producer of Australia's best Cabernet Sauvignon wines, Chardonnay, Sauvignon Blanc, and Riesling.

New South Wales is a major wine production area from which much of the locally commercial Chardonnay and Shiraz is historically produced. Recent droughts have seen increased experimenting with varieties that are more drought friendly, such as Verdelho and Tempranillo.

Victoria is the major wine production location, but prominent growing areas have cooler climates and are nearer Melbourne.

Wine away:
From wine tasting day trips to wine holidays the world over

Where the word "wine" originated, remains a mystery. Despite being similar to many early language versions of the word, the root of wine as a word probably grew out of win-, from a long-forgotten and ancient Mediterranean language

Wine can well be observed as a holiday in a bottle, this is a fact, and very much all in the perspective of the imbiber. Why restrict yourself to discovering new wines from the comfort of home when you can be day tripping or journeying around the world, enjoying all it has to offer the wine lovers? Wine tourism is a real thing. There is even a choice of words that are dictionary worthy which describe the concept. Enotourism, oenotourism, and vinitourism all lend credence to this fairly new addition to the tourism world. The purpose of this particularly attractive holiday embraces the tasting, consumption and buying of wine, preferably from or near the source. Where tourism by its very nature is typically passive in nature, vinitourism includes visiting wineries, tasting wines, strolls through vineyards, and, for the more fortunate, even actively participating in the harvesting. Enotourism even has its own holiday, celebrated on the second Sunday of November every year.

Wine tours are an option around which to create a holiday. The wine gods know as well as any mere mortal that the best holiday destinations are also prime wine producing regions on this bountiful earth we are fortunate enough to call home. Wine always seems to taste a whole lot better when it is sipped and savoured straight from the cellar door, so choose a destination and book a wine sabbatical.

Make a holiday of it, why not? To encourage this concept even further, I bet you did not know that there is in fact a wine drinking calendar. Yes sir, I kid you not. Although none of these days are recognized anywhere globally as a dinkum holiday, and your employer will likely not give you any of the days off, they are nonetheless pertinent. Somewhere in the world, throughout the world, there is a legitimate reason to be enjoying wine. Let's have a closer look, shall we...

February has not one, but a few reasons. And why should it not? It is after all either pretty cold or pretty hot around this time of year, depending on where on Earth you find yourself. So here's February in a nutshell:

February 18th: Drink Wine Day "spread the love and health benefits of wine" on this day.

February 27th: Open That Bottle Night to celebrate opening that special ambrosia you have tucked away for the right time.

Which turns out to be around February month end every year, but the actual day does change. Who knew!?

February 1st to 28th (or 29th, depending) *Delaware Wine Month*. Yes, all month!

Marching on....

March 3rd: National Mulled Wine Day. Need we say more?

The month of Autumn or Spring... depending, y'know

April 17th: World Malbec Day serves opportunity to raise your glass and toast the Argentine Malbec.

All month: Michigan Wine Month Cheers!

Yes, you May...

May 6th: International Sauvignon Blanc Day. Salut!

May 9th: World Moscato Day. Sweet!

May 16th: Granholm vs. Heald Anniversary, a celebration of the law that insisted 'more wine!".

May 26th: National Chardonnay Day. Although the dates might differ year to year, the celebration of oaked or unoaked remains steadfast.

May 24th: Anniversary of the Judgment of Paris, or "slurp heard round the world" the celebrates Californian beating French in the wine tasting competition.

May 25th: National Wine Day closely following on the inebriated heels of February's National Drink Wine Day

May: Oregon Wine Month because sometimes a day just won't cut it.

Just June and we're halfway through the year, so it brings you not one but two Wine Month occasions:

All month! Idaho Wine Month AND Ohio Wine Month.

July seems to take a mid-year wine break of its own, but August comes back with a winegeance...

August 1st: International Albarino Day because every month should have a varietal day if it can. August celebrates this lively, crisp white.

August 14th: International Rosé Day, which may or may not actually be around mid-June, so when uncertainty presents, just revel in Rosé on both occasions.

August 18th: National Pinot Noir Day, who said a varietal rejoice should be limited to once a month?

All month! August is of course Washington Wine Month.

Somewhere betwixt August and September, always the last Thursday before Labour Day, rejoice in Cabernet Day.

But September is celebration month for California, Missouri, North Carolina, AND Illinois, who all have it as their Wine Months! Here's to September – raise a glass, again and again and again...

September whenever the 3rd Friday falls: International Grenache Day.

October 11-17th: Drink Local Wine Week Do we need any more reason?

October 23rd: Champagne Day because bubbles should be cheered and shared!

All month it's Wine Month in Texas, Virginia, and Pennsylvania.

Two months to go...

November 7th: International Merlot Day.

November 12th: Wine Tourism Day seems the ideal time to plan that break we discussed at the start of this chapter.

November 12th: International Tempranillo Day.

November 18th: National Zinfandel Day is not just another varietal celebration but of "America's heritage grape."

2nd Sunday of November: "Enotourism Day" promotes cellar visits in Germany, Austria, Slovenia, Spain, France, Greece, Hungary, Italy, and Portugal

The best of celebration months....

December 4th: Cabernet Franc Day.

December 5th: Repeal Day is commemorated with a drink or two since 1933.

December 20th: National Sangria Day because a wine enjoyed with infused fruit is great no matter the season.

December 31st: National Champagne Day for all the right reasons.

**Now that we have the reasons and the seasons,
let's take a gander at where to holiday.**

"Around the World in 80 Vines: A Wine Tour Around the World" offers a 4-day trip departing from and ending in London, visiting 15 wine regions around the world.

Begin in France with the world's finest vineyards, with a 6-night stay in Provence and an overnight in Chateauneuf Du Pape. Then it's a 2-night stay in Rioja, Spain, the picturesque Tuscany, Italy for 2 nights, and Mount Etna, Italy for another 2 nights. Experience the unusual wine regions with 2 nights each in Cricova in Moldova and Transylvania, Romania, 5 nights in Nashik, India, 2 nights in both Margaret River and Barossa Valley in Australia, 4 nights in Queenstown, New Zealand, Napa Valley, USA for 3 nights, Elqui Valley, Chile for 2 nights, Mendoza, Argentina for 3 nights and lastly 3 nights in the Western Cape, South Africa.

"Loire Valley Chateaux Day Tour" offers wine lovers a full day opportunity to discover the landscapes of the Loire Valley, taste regional wines and cuisine, and visit two magnificent châteaux or wineries.

"Small-Group Day Tour of Loire Valley"

Joint visits to 3 of the Loire Valley chateaux as a participant of this small-group trip: Chenoceau for wine tastings and lunch, le Clos Lucé, and the Amboise Royal Castle.

Here's what to expect:

You'll depart from the designated pick-up point and arrive at Chenoceau. Tour the chateau's unique architecture, take a stroll through the renaissance-style gardens learning about the history of the castle. Explore a cellar cave which dates back to 1874 and experience the fruits of the mature Vouvray wines before lunching on a traditional French meal at a local restaurant for. The Royal Castle of Amboise gives an up close and personal look at the transitioning of Gothic to Renaissance architecture. View the grave of Leonardo da Vinci in the chapel and visit the Chateau of the Clos Lucé, where da Vinci spent his final years.

"Napa Valley Wine Train" day tour offers wine lovers the opportunity to explore the best of Napa and Sonoma Valleys. This package includes 3-hour journey aboard the vintage Wine Train, visits to 4 wineries, breakfast, lunch, and a gourmet dinner. The first stop is at Jacuzzi Family Vineyards, the breath-taking winery with an old-world feel and far-reaching vineyard views that offers more than just wine. Drive through the gently rolling hills and sweeping flat plains of Carneros, a wine-growing region and sub-appellation tucked in between the Napa and Sonoma Valleys. Carneros is sheep in Spanish and was known for the many sheep ranches dotting the hillsides. Today you will note that more than 20 wineries call this region home, portraying more a European feel than Californian. Although you will still see sheep. Amble and shop downtown Napa and the Oxbow Public Market before embarking on your exquisite culinary adventure through the stunning Napa Valley aboard the train awaiting you at the Wine Train Station.

"Wine Enthusiast Tour" is a day tour departing from Paris, where you'll discover and taste French wines enjoying somewhat more prestige than most. A t the crossroads of Loire-Valley and Burgundy, learn about the region, its traditions and its Pinot Noir, Sauvignon and Chardonnay wines. Sample the iconic "Crottin de Chavignol" goat cheese at a working cheese farm, visit two vineyards in the Pouilly-Fumé and Sancerre regions and meet the passionate winemakers welcoming you to taste their wines. Visit caves and fermentation process rooms; explore the fields of vines and sit down to a classic French set luncheon menu in a quaint local village restaurant.

"Chianti afternoon Wine Tour" is a 6-hour Chianti wine tour from Florence, through the Tuscan countryside, past olive groves, vineyards and rolling hills, to enjoy of the most prestigious winemaking regions in the world. Visit two wineries in scenic villages in the Chianti Fiorentino and Chianti Senese regions to taste their most appreciated Tuscan wines, learn their characteristics, explore the wine cellars and hear the winemakers' secrets. Afterward, head to the medieval village of Greve, where the most important wine fair of the Chianti region is held each year, explore the main square and the local artisan shops. Continue to the family-run winery to be found in the Sienese area. Join the winemaker in a guided tour of the cellars and then head into the garden to enjoy four wines and local products. The days ends in Castellina, a hilltop village characterised by its large fortress and Etruscan settlements.

Stellenbosch Region - Daily tours invites you to visit 5 estates in and around Stellenbosch. This university town is of the oldest settlements in South Africa, well-renowned for Cape Dutch style architecture. All farms on this route are selected to allow an experience of iconic estates as well as family run farms. You'll get the opportunity to visit 5 wine estates, pair locally produced, world-class cheeses, and learn the art of wine tasting, food and wine pairing, and how to order wine at restaurants. Included is lunch in the wine lands and samplings of a varied range of wine styles, local treats of cured meats and artisanal chocolate paired with selected wines.

Franschhoek/Stellenbosch wine tour kicks off with a morning drive through Stellenbosch with a cellar tour and wine & chocolate pairing followed by an intimate cheese & wine pairing at a boutique wine estate. Cross the picturesque Stellenbosch mountains onto the cuisine capital of South Africa, Franschhoek. It is here where the French Huguenots settled and caused South Africa to earn a place in wine history. After a tasting at an award-winning estate, you're treated to a Franschhoek lunch and a chance to stroll about before a wine tasting along the mountain foothills before heading back to Cape Town.

Champagne Trip and Tasting at Moët & Chandon or Feuillatte is a day trip from Paris to the Champagne region of France for an opportunity to taste the world's finest bubbly, beginning in the delightful village of Éparnay. Perambulate the village, home to the modernistic Nicolas Feuillatte House and the more traditional Moët & Chandon cellars. After your first Champagne tasting of the day, explore the streets and partake in a locally produced lunch at the Avenue de Champagne. A drive through the hillside vineyards will reveal why this village is celebrated as the birthplace of Champagne, with its medieval Benedictine monastery from whence the inspired monk, Dom Pérignon, made his effervescent discovery. At the medieval winery of Veuve Clicquot, witness how the grapes are transformed from the vines into award-winning champagnes. The tour culminates on the terraces overlooking the vineyards, sipping champagne before hopping on the private bus back to Paris.

Paris wine tasting on location in central Paris is the wine tasting tour de France option just minutes from the Louvre. Taste the wines all the different regions of France have to offer to discover the difference between wine produced in Champagne, Bordeaux, Sancerre and the Rhone. Your sommelier will teach you how Champagne is made, how to taste wine properly, the styles of wine, how to read a French label, and clarify concepts like terroir and appellation on this virtual tour through the prominent wine regions of France. If you choose to remain for dinner, the O Chateau's wine bar offers delicious delights and 40 wines to try by the glass.

Northern Rhône Tournon-sur-Rhône and Hermitage Tour is a cost-effective how-do-you-do of the deep-flavoured wines of tis particularly wineish region. Including hotel stays, the tour spoils with Tain l'Hermitage and the boutique of Paul Jaboulet Aîne wine tastings, and a traditional three course luncheon. Climb Hérmitage Hill to walk off the feasts of the tour and enjoy breath-taking views across the Rhône valley from "La Chapelle." Choose to spend a second night in Tournon sur Rhône to better experience all the region has to offer.

Rhône by Train Wine Tour is a six-day Rhône Valley experience beginning with a train trip between Lyon Part Dieu and Condrieu, a quaint village on the river. Overnight at the foot of the vineyards overlooking the river in the Beau Rivage hotel and end the first day with a four-course dinner. A full day dawns to enjoy Ampuis and the Côte Rôtie producer and the train journey to Tain L'Hérmitage. This precedes the two-night's accommodation across the river in Tournon-sur-Rhône, at the inviting boutique hotel, la Villéon. Across the river, you will be welcomed at the Paul Jaboulet Aîné boutique in the village of Tain L'Hérmitage. Taste two Hérmitage reds, the latest vintage of "La Chapelle" among them, as well as the Hérmitage white wine and then savour a three-course luncheon accompanied by a couple of Jaboulet wines. St Péray or Cornas winery rounds off the day of touring. The final leg of the tour starts with a train trip to, and hotel accommodation in, Avignon. Visit the Papal Palace and Pont d'Avignon, and partake in drinks and a four-course dinner before bedding down for the night. Tours and tastings at the villages of Gigondas, Châteauneuf-du-Pape, and Vacqueyras, are finished off with a luncheon at a local bistrot.

Simply Avignon, Southern Rhône Wine tour is another low-cost introduction option to the wines of the Southern Rhône. It starts with an early evening wine tasting of three Southern Rhône wines accompanied by cheese and meat platters in an authentic tasting boutique. A half day transported tour of the world-famous Châteauneuf-du-Pape appellation to discover the unusual terroir precedes tours and tastings at two wineries before returning to Avignon. A visit to a Châteauneuf-du-Pape winery and a tour of the Roman amphitheatre in Orange may be included.

Lyon & Rhône Valley Wine Tour over five days is a fantastic to explore the Northern Rhône, with added opportunities to indulge in the unique local cuisine of, and overnight in Lyon (also known as the City of Lights). Experience also Tain l'Hermitage and Tournon-sur-Rhône, surrounded by the charming vineyards of the Northern Rhône. Enjoy drinks and a three-course dinner at a traditional Bouchon Lyonnais, the likes of which can only be experienced in Lyon, where restaurants serve traditional Lyonnaise food in a welcoming atmosphere.

Lyons is discovered magnanimously in a four-hour walking tour which not only gives you opportunity to shed those pounds after the night before but allows you to enjoy Lyon's historic district. Lyon's odd passageways called Traboules, which means "to cross" in Latin, were used for centuries by the locals of the city and by the silk workers, to transport fabrics from workshops to merchants. Taste the local delicacies at the many shops before a relaxing evening of doing whatever pleases you best. It is said that the moonlight in these parts is unsurpassed when enjoyed with the right companions.

At Lyon-Part-Dieu station, board the train to Tain l'Hermitage to overnighting across the river in French hospitality in Tournon-sur-Rhône, enjoying enviable views over the Hermitage Hills. Tour the local winery of Tain l'Hermitage and the Paul Jaboulet Aîné boutique where the three-course lunch is accompanied by two Jaboulet wines. Five Syrah wines are just waiting for you at the tasting at the respected Chapoutier thereafter.

Fun and Quite Interesting Facts to Sip on

Charles Gordon Maynard wanted to make sweets to savour like a fine wine, and wine gums were born. Naming these after port, sherry, champagne, burgundy and claret was merely a ruse as their flavourings are derived only from fruit

There is more to wine than just the drinking. This is arguable, but nonetheless, regardless of your views on the subject, we can interest you in some funny, interesting and timeless verities to digest and enjoy.

Grapes ferment sans additional sugars, enzymes, water, acids, or other nutrients, because of a natural chemical balance.

People with a hatred of or fear of wine suffer from oenophobia.

The English invented the dark green wine bottle in the 1600's. Who knows, if it were not invented by Sir Kenelm Digby wine might still be stored in goat skin bags.

Wine 'tastings' are so named quite erroneously. It is widely agreed among Sommeliers that the smell is the most important sense when drinking wines.

On average, the age of French oaks trees cut for making wine barrels is 170 years, and around 400 species of oak trees are used for the making of oak wine barrels.

The main fruit grown during the 1940's in Napa Valley was not grapes but prunes.

There are currently ten thousand wine grape varieties present worldwide.

When toasting the signing of the Declaration of Independence, Madeira was the wine drunk.

A "cork-tease" is a person who talks incessantly or often about opening a certain wine, but never does.

Wine may well have health benefits, but it is believed to also nominally increase the likelihood of particular forms of cancer of the digestive tract and most specifically cancer of the oesophagus.

Non-European wines are named after grape varieties while their European counterparts get their names from their geographic locations.

Two dominant medieval institutions besides churches and monasteries, more precisely universities and hospitals, glean the majority of their earnings from wine.

Eiswein is a wine made from frozen grapes, which was invented by the Germans.

A red wine that is permitted to become too warm may risk its fruity flavour, and chilling a wine minimises its sweetness.

By burning sulphur candles inside the empty wine containers, the Romans discovered that they were kept fresh and free of a vinegary smell.

The word "sommelier" means an officer in charge of supplies, or a butler, and is from the old French word which originates from the Old Provençal word saumalier.

When planting new vines, the first harvests will only be ready in four to five years.

The word butt originates in medieval times and denotes the measurement used to determine the liquid volume of wine.

During the Prohibition years, the wine industry in the United States of America was immensely impacted, taking many years to recover after it was abolished. Those wineries which survived through these years did so by taking advantage of the loophole in the very restrictive law which allowed for the production of ceremonial wine for religious reasons.

The corkscrew was first conspired of in the middle of the 19th century. Not as old as you suspected, is it?

The sugar naturally found in grapes is converted into alcohol and carbon dioxide with the help of a yeast, which is a single-celled organism very helpful in the wine making process during which heat is released.

Wine glasses are generally specifically shaped to direct wine to key areas of the nose and tongue, emphasising central features of the beverage, so that it can be best appreciated and fully enjoyed.

While wines ae all stored at the same temperature for best results, the reds and the whites are enjoyed at very different temperatures.

A glass of wine is made from the juice of just a single cluster of grapes, which is around 75 grapes in total.

Before cork was used for a wine stopper, oil-soaked rags were stuffed into the bottles.

Ten bottles of wine are produced from a single grape vine.

Wine is not made from the typical table grapes to be found at the store. Wine grapes, known by the Latin term Vitis vinifera, are thick skinned, small, and sweet, and have seeds. There are over a thousand grape varieties.

Of all the beverages known to man, wine is the oldest.

Archaeologists found grape seeds dating from 8 000 B.C. in Jordan, Turkey, Syria, and Lebanon, which indicated evidence of wine. Georgia was the site of the findings of the oldest pips belonging to cultivated vines, dating way back to between 7 000 and 5 000 BC.

A glass of red wine has about 85 calories.

Hippocrates is commonly considered the father of medicine. In the writings of what would one day become known as modern-day prescriptions, almost all of his that have been found and recorded prescribe wine as a cure for sick patients.

The only book in the Old Testament of the Bible that has no reference to the vine or wine is the Book of Jonah.

Jesus performed his first miracle at the wedding feast, when he turned water into wine.

Cork is the eco-friendliest wine stopper and the cork for the majority of wine bottle corks is harvested in Portugal which boasts 33% of the 2,200,000 hectares of cork forest around the world.

The Cistercians and Benedictines of the monastic orders were by far the best and most innovative winemakers of the day during the Middle Ages. Quite appropriately, they were known to actually taste the earth to determine changes in the soil changed from place to place. The findings going back to this long-ago time are still pertinent and important in modern times.

Since the antioxidants found in red wine lower the incidence of type-2 diabetes, heart disease, and very finally death, it can be agreed that moderate drinking of red wine in small doses is healthier than teetotalling.

The plant pigment anthocyanin found in grape skins is responsible for giving red wine its hue.

As red wines age, so it becomes lighter in colour.

Red wine grapes can produce white wine. Because the colour does not come from the juice but from the grape skins, white wine can be produced from red grapes. This can be achieved by making the wine in the same way as normal but eliminating contact with the grape skins. For example, the white sparkling wine Blanc de Noirs Champagne is produced from with Pinot Meunier and Pinot Noir grapes, which are red.

A wine barrel holds 60 gallons of wine, that is over 227 litres.

Many people commonly refer to grapes as a fruit, but botanists technically classify grapes as berries since each fruit forms from a single flower.

La lutte raisonnée means 'the reasoned struggle' and these wines are typically referred to as organic wines. These wines are distinguished by a ladybird logo in assorted forms. Wine growers practicing this form of viticulture are motivated by a less aggressive use of chemicals than conventional growers.

Vineyards cover around 7.5 million hectares or 18 million acres across the globe, with Spain, China, France, Italy, Turkey, and the United States being the top grape growing countries.

Research shows that white wines are beneficial to lung tissues as it keeps them healthy.

Wines aren't just red or white: some unique wines are golden, pink, or even orange.

A Nebuchadnezzar is the name of an oversized wine bottle. A Nebuchadnezzar holds the equivalent of twenty 750-milliliter bottles of wine while a magnum holds 1,500 millilitres of wine, the equivalent of two standard wine bottles.

Grapes grown in sandy soil generally produce less acidic, softer wine, while soils with a lot of clay produce wines with deep, bold flavours.

One should refrain from ordering the second cheapest wine on a menu. This is a much-known life hack and will not fool anyone at the table into believing that you know anything about wine or that you are not in fact merely a cheapskate. Rather op for asking the sommelier for suggestions. It is not uncommon for restaurants to price lesser known varieties more alluringly to encourage diners to try the unknown.

Terroir is an important player in wine making worldwide. The term refers to the natural features of a body of land, which include topography, climate, geology and soil, and the manner in which these intermingle and work together to form the unique and specific characteristics of the wines produced within the area.

FAQs about wine drinking

Drinking wine is a great cure for keeping things bottled up

Can you suggest any sweet wines?

Those with incredibly sensitive taste buds may prefer the taste of sweet wines over those with a harsher taste. Taste vary for sweet wines, which are not only suitable for dessert. You cannot go wrong with Vouvray, Sauternes, Muscat, Chenin Blanc, Icewine, Tokaji, Riesling, and any Port or late harvest wine.

At what temperature should wine best be served?

Ideally, red wine: 65°F/18°C; white & rosé wine 55°F/13°C; Champagne & other bubbly at 45°F/7°C. Keep Reds in a closet or a cool cellar to maintain these ideal temperatures. Refrigerate Whites and Rosés. Bubblies should be cooled for longer or you could make use of an ice bucket.

Why does wine sometimes have a hint of vanilla in its flavour?

Newish oak barrels will give the wine stored in it that vanilla flavour and aroma.

For how long can I store wine and what is needed for best results?

Wines should ideally be drunk within a year of their release on the market, or ideally within another year or two. At least 90% of wines should be enjoyed young. White wines are not typically cellared for extended periods of time. The very best Sauternes and Graves are specific exceptions to this rule, however. The finest Red Wines can be kept cloistered in the cellar for many decades, and reds are usually cellared for lengthier periods. The vintage and the type of grape used in the wine making make a big difference in the storing of wines.

How should left over wine be stored for the best results?

The key point to saving leftover wine is to keep it free of oxygen. Degradation soon occurs when wine is allowed to oxidise. Store leftovers in a small receptable to the point that it is almost overflowing. Cork or plug the container so that wine doesn't spill out, in this way you will ensure that no air bubbles present in the container. Refrigerate and only remove the receptable when you want to partake of the pleasures of the vibe once more. At this time, allow it to warm to the desired temperature for drinking. Wine can be thus stored for no longer than five to seven days, depending on whether white or red. Left over wine retained for cooking purposes can be frozen in ice cube trays and then kept in airtight freezer bags for use in dining pleasures such as sauces.

Why does white wine not cause my mouth to feel dry like red wine does?

This is due to the tannic element. White wine have less of it than do Red wines. Since the tannins are as a result of the grape skins, and the juice in red wines are softened for a period of time with the stems, seeds and skins of the grapes, the greater extract of tannins makes Reds higher in content than whites which are typically immediately pressed of the skins.

How much wine is in a standard bottle?

That would be 750ml.

IS there a reason that people slurp wine?

Wine professional will slurp wine for much the same reason as others swirl wine in the glass, although the behaviour is more intense. Both behaviours lead to the introduction of oxygen to the wine. Slurping the wine through the mouth and swirling the wine in the glass serve to open aromas, allowing different flavours opportunity to present

What is an organic wine?

Today many meticulous viticulturists go all out to use less chemicals in their vineyards. The French term for this is *lutte raisoné* which is loosely translated to a rational battle against the issues of fungus, insects, and weeds. Organic viticulture is different with stricter regulations that serve to hold producers to the use of only naturally occurring products as pest control. These mindful wine producers monitor the levels of pest and weed presentation and only spray if it is absolutely called for.

How many bottles of wine will I get in a case of wine?

Twelve bottles make up a case. That totals 9 litres of the good stuff per case.

Is wine good for you?

Regular and moderate consumption of wine is good for you, if research is to be believed. Red wine in particular apparently reduces the danger of coronary heart disease. The cholesterol that blocks arteries is low-density lipoprotein cholesterol (LPD) and these are cleared from the blood by high-density lipoprotein cholesterol (HPD). Moderate alcohol consumption produces a better balance of the two and alcohol has a blood thinner effect which makes blood less likely to clot. There is also evidence that wine can reduce the risk of developing Alzheimer's disease or having a stroke.

How many calories does a glass of wine have?

A glass of dry red or white wine has about 110 calories. Sweeter wine with lingering sugar as well as alcohol has more calories. The higher the alcohol content, the higher the number of calories.

What does "oaky" mean? What is it that causes a wine to be oaky?

A wine that has a flavour reminiscent of wood or oak is called oaky. This flavour comes through in wines that are fermented and/or aged in oak barrels.

IS the shape of the wine bottle any indicator of the quality of its contents?

There are certainly historically traditional colours and bottle shapes that come into play for the different wine styles. For wine that should not be left to age, clear glass bottles are the preference. Coloured glass serves to present the wine from darkening due to over exposure to bright light, and it also filters the harmful rays. Brown glass is usually the keeper of sweeter wines. Green bottles are mostly reserved for a Dry. German style bottles are more slender and typically assigned to sweeter, fruitier wines. Wider burgundy bottles hold the dry whites, typically Chardonnay. Dark brown bottles are preferred for Ports, with a longish neck and very square shoulders. Earthy reds are usually to be found bottled in burgundy-shaped bottles, favoured for Pinot Noir, and more square-shouldered claret bottles for red blends containing Cabernet, Sauvignon Blanc, and Cabernet Sauvignon.

How Do I Select the Right Glass in which to Serve Wine?

You can drink your wine from any glass you like, however there are some thoughts that may useful when selecting wine glasses. Clear glass allows you to see the colour and clarity of the wine. Glass is a poor conductor of heat which is a plus, keeping the wine from warming quicker when held in the hand. Red wine is usually served a few degrees warmer than white wine, so a glass for red wine should preferably have a well-rounded bottom to provide warming contact between the hand and the wine. White wine is usually served chilled, so a long-stemmed glass will keep the hands away from the wine. The actual bowl of the glass could also be narrowed down to a point. For sparkling wine use a champagne flute, tall and slim, with only a very small surface area. This way the bubbles will last longer. Never fill any wine glass, especially a red wine glass, to the brim, as this doesn't allow the drinker to nose the wine properly without dipping his or her nose in it.

Once my wine bottle is open, how long should it remain drinkable?

Oxidation is the enemy of wine, and it gets a hold the moment the cork is removed from the bottle. Refrigeration may hamper its progress but will definitely not stop oxidation from progressing. By transferring the wine to a smaller receptable which allows less exposure to oxygen, it should last longer.

I have found crystals on the bottom of my cork. What are they?

The tartrate crystals look very much like shards of glass, but it is a natural and thoroughly benign manifestation. The crystals are odourless and tasteless and made up of the same substance as crème of tartar.

Where are the best value wines from?

One word: Chile. Especially their Sauvignon Blanc and Cabernet Sauvignon. South Africa notably their also Sauvignon Blanc, Argentina, notably Malbec, and New Zealand, also Sauvignon Blanc are also great value.

What wines is best to serve at a large gathering or party?

With White wines you can't really go wrong with either New Zealand or Chilean Sauvignon Blanc. For a red, either Argentina's Malbec or a cru Beaujolais, such as Fleurie. When wanting a cost-effective bubbly to serve to a group the Cava from Spain is always a winner.

Funny or Weird Wine Labels

Drink a bottle of wine to stay focused

It is termed *Drinking with your Eyes*, and is big business for designers of those alluring, interesting and very often quirky labels that cause you to reach into the shelf and add the bottle to your take-home selection. A wine label must attract the attention of the peruser, drawing the eye to their bottle and away from the hundreds of similar options on the shelves. That is after all its purpose. That and to inform about the wine behind the label. It is the label that tricks the buyer into splurging on that bottle that is just out of the budget, but did you notice how expensive it looks? It just has to be good and a steal at that price... A label that indicates better value will always sell its product better. Labels are all about subliminal. Also the whimsical are attractive. We all know that wine tasting is more than just tasting – it harnesses all the senses. This harnessing starts with the label when you ae looking to select a bottle off the shelf.

Some labels manage to do this way more eloquently than most.

Fat Bastard came about when French wine maker Thierry Boudinard used his newly acquired vocabulary fresh from a visit to Australia on visiting Guy Anderson, saying "Taste zis fat bastard".

Marilyn Merlot presents on a label featuring Marilyn Monroe's image, and is best appreciated when spoken in an American drawl. It comes from Nova Wines by Marilyn Monroe's estate.

The Hunting Ghost is not only attention grabbing in the alluring wording itself but also in the way in which the white font against pitch black lends a haunting feel. How many of you noticed the missing 'a' assumed by the reader to be in the label?

Blue Hugs just invites drinking with company, does it not? The hands in inviting form being the only form of image on the label serves to accentuate the hug.

Arrogant Frog can be appreciated as a play on the wine originating from a humble French winemaker with a sense of humour.

The Ball Buster wine was initially named "Michelle's Block" after the wife of the winemaker. A punchier and more eye-catching label was required, though, and after some brainstorming over how the industry caused blood, sweat and tears and could bust your balls, the 'buy me' label was born.

Smoking Parrot is a cheaper wine playing on the label of the notoriously expensive Pouilly Fume Loire wine. Let's break it down: Polly (sounds like Pouilly) is another name for a parrot. Fume is French for 'smoke'. Voila!

Frog's Piss because of France's synonymity with frogs…. Oui, it is a French Red.

Cleavage Creek – Napa Valley- features the image of a respectably full-bodied cleavage on the label to give impetus to the not too subtle point. Napa Valley is said to produce grapes from the cleavage of some of California's most beautiful hills. Proceeds from sales benefit breast cancer research.

Sheila's Chardonnay - although Bruce did help (a bit) – From the Fair Dinkum Winery is worth buying just to read the full label which goes on to proclaim, 'no sheep were harmed during the making of this fine wine'.

BONUS:
Food and Wine Journal - Pairing Wine with Meals

Remarkable Wine Label:
The Ball Buster -Barossa Valley-

Wine and food pairings is all about balance. The wine must neither masque the food, nor the food hide the wine. Pairing the right wine with your meal can be a bit tricky and understandably overwhelming, especially for one who is new to the world of wine. With such a vast selection, choosing the wrong wine could more than possibly ruin the meal. Why do we do it, though? Optimal wine and food pairing initiates some equilibrium between the elements of a dish and the features of a wine. That's the short story.

While this wine and food appears complex, the basics are reassuringly simple to follow. Wines should be more acidic than the food or sweeter than the food.

The wine should have the same flavour intensity as the food.

Red wines pair best with bold flavoured meats, such as red meat.

White wines pair best with light-intensity meats, such as chicken or fish.

Bitter wines, typically the reds, are best balanced with fat.

Opt rather to pair the wine and the sauce than the wine with the meat.

The norm is that, White, Sparkling and Rosé wines create contrasting pairings while Red wines create congruent pairings. Of course this is rather the rule than a must and wine is dripping with exceptions.

If the matter of contrasting pairings requires more explanation, here it is. This takes some practice, so make it a fun exercise over time. Serve a light wine when the food is dense and a dry wine with food that is sweet. Try contrasting every aspect for the best results if you are going to be successful at this kind of pairing. Complement pairings are wonderful when serving a single course at a dinner party followed by a dessert. In this situation, your palate has the chance to savour the bolder flavours of the main course and wine pairing. Instead of then being bored by the same again, shake up the taste buds with a follow-up sweeter pairing that once again excites the palate.

Let us now get down to the nitty gritty of the matter.

Pinot Noir pairs rather well with earthy flavours, in other words ingredients such as mushrooms and truffles.

Chardonnay pairs well with chicken, pasta, seafood, fatty fish or fish in a rich sauce.

Champagne becomes sweeter when paired with salty foods.

Bordeaux and Cabernet Sauvignon pair extremely well with red meats, such as steaks or chops, and the tannins clear the palate after every bite.

Sauvignon Blanc pairs with raw or lightly cooked foods, such as sushi, grilled fish or tangy foods.

Dry rosé can be paired with any cheesy dish, while only some cheeses pair with white wine and some with red. This is because dry rosé has the acidity of white wine and the fruit character of red.

Malbec, Shiraz and Côtes-du-Rhône are bold enough to drink with foods that are heavily spiced, such as barbecue sauces.

Moderately sweet sparkling wines such as demi-sec (semi dry) Champagne emphasise the fruit in desserts instead of the sugar.

Syrah, which has spicy characteristics, pairs well with highly spiced dishes.

Riesling and Gewürztraminer have a slight sweetness to them which helps tame spicy dishes, such as curries. Therefore, pairing this wine with sweet and spicy dishes is advised. A sweet wine also pairs well with sour and salty foods, and puddings the likes of butterscotch, caramel or fruit.

Rosé wines, Rosé Champagne, and sparkling wines pair ingeniously with a great variety of main course meals. One can't go wrong with this wine as an accompaniment to dinner.

Pasta with a tomato-based sauce should be paired with any bold Red, such as Cabernet or Malbec, while pasta with a white sauce should be paired with medium or light wines, such as Rosé or rich Whites.

Specifics on Wine Pairings for Various Meals and Occasions

It can all seem rather daunting, and understandably so. Even for those wine connoisseurs among us, the very idea of satisfying all guests at a meal can seem hopelessly unachievable. Serving a wine that will be acceptable to the likes of the culinarily particular Aunt Lydia as well as Great Uncle Bob, who imbibes a little more than is appreciated by the rest of the family, can strike apprehension in most anyone. Every guest list has one or more, and the trick is to handle the situation with an air of confidence. Keep it simple and follow these basic guidelines and Bob's you uncle, so to say.

Cheese and Wine

It just would not have been a pairing discussion without the cheese and wine. Feel free to experiment here. Since cheese and wine usually rounds off a meal, bring in whatever wine is left over from the meal. If the evening is just a cheese and wine, play around with your options, using some base pointers.

As a novice, try pairing wine and cheese from the same **location**.

There is also much to be said or local traditions when it comes to wine pairing. Wine and cheese have after all come a long way and been around a great deal longer than you or I. When in Spain.... Garnacha wines complement Spanish Manchego with its candied and fruity flavours. The French Loire Valley brings you the Sauvignon Blanc that goes great with goat cheese. The Portuguese island of Madeira brings you Madeira, a fortified wine with tangy nuttiness and fruit-cake aromas and smoky, toffee flavours which is delightful with sheep's milk. The high acidity of Madeira cuts through the richness of full-fat firm brebis cheese, Cabrales, and Etorki, and enhances its flavours. And we have already touched on the pairing of Burgundy's Chardonnay with Époisses de Bourgogne.

Fresh Cheeses are soft and have no rind. These are mild with a slightly tangy flavour and include Ricotta, Mozzarella, Mascarpone, very young Selles sur Cher, Stracchino, Boursin, Burrata, Feta, and Chèvre. Pair with young, fruity, unoaked red wines, crisp, dry, young and off dry white bottlings, and crisp, dry rosé wine. Think white with Pinot Blanc, Albariño, Sauvignon Blanc, young Chardonnay, Soave, Vermentino, Muscadet, Verdejo, Arneis, Gewürztraminer or Riesling. For red wines, Pinot Noir, Gamay, Loire Cabernet Franc, Zweigelt, and Valpolicella.

Strong, firm cheeses such as aged Manchego or Pecorino and, Gouda and Cheddar, Provolone, Gruyère, and Parmesan-style varieties are complemented by bold Red wines - Syrah, Tempranillo, Cabernet Sauvignon, Sangiovese, Merlot, and Zinfandel. As cheese ages, it loses water content and gains flavour with the added fat content.

Creamy, soft cheeses the likes of Muenster, Camembert, Brie, Cremont, or Époisses de Bourgogne are perfectly suited to

Sparkling wine, with its palate cleansing abilities. Champagne and Prosecco are of course included here. If the fizz isn't what you are after, try the Chardonnay. Any Burgundian Chablis, and moderately or unoaked styles will let the cheese flavours through while cutting through the rich creaminess with its subtlety and acidity. Dry, light-bodied Sauvignon Blanc, young Riesling, and dry Chenin Blanc will be suitable white wines. Textured white Rhône varieties are great with ripe, pungent cheese, specifically Châteauneuf-du-Pape Blanc but also Marsanne and Roussanne. For reds, go with the young, dry and light-bodied wines that are fruity and unoaked, such as Pinot Noir, Cabernet Franc from the Loire, Bonarda, Gamay, Zweigelt, Dolcetto, Barbera, and Mencía.

Stinky Cheese such as Stinking Bishop, Munster, and Livarot and any blue veined cheeses that have strong flavours are best appreciated with the strong spicy and floral bouquets of Gewürztraminer, off-dry Riesling and Viognier. Sweeter wines like Late Harvest dessert wines, Moscato, and Port are another great option. Sauternes is delectably paired with Roquefort. Port pairs deliciously with Stilton, in particular and also blue cheese, not because it is red but because it is fortified and sweet. The sweetness of Port perfectly foils the cheese's tangy saltiness. Blue veined cheeses pair well with Austrian or German late harvest wine and sweet wines such as Tokaji and Icewine.

Firm, nutty cheese. You cannot go wrong with cheeses like Emmental, Gouda, Gruyère, Swiss, Abbaye de Belloc, and Comté Extra when you're a little unsure of what do drink with what. These cheeses can be enjoyed with white or red wine. So feel liberated.

Now that we have that paired and packed away, we can get down to a certain nitty gritty of food and wine pairing examples.

Sample Menu 1:
Three course Italian Meal

You cannot beat an Italian meal when pairing wine. They simply go together like the proverbial horse and carriage.

When serving **antipasto**, go for the Italian **Pinot Grigio**. This white wine, born and perfected in Italy, it is a dry wine, whereas French Pinot Grigio and Pinot Gris from Alsace are slightly sweet.

Flavours: robust but simple. White nectarine, lemon, lime, pear, and apple. Some regions may produce a light honey flavour.

Bouquet: although not extraordinarily significantly flavoured, florals such as honeysuckle are present as well as a saline-like minerality.

Il Primo: For the **first course**, Italian meatballs and pasta with a rich, tomato-based sauce beg for a tangy and bold red wine, such as **Zinfandel**.

Flavours: cherry, plum, boysenberry, blackberry, strawberry, peach, liquorice, sweet tobacco and cinnamon.

Bouquet: liquorice, star anise, black pepper, cardamom, and smoke.

Il Secondo: This is the main dish of the meal and let us pretend we are dining in a coastal region of Italy and serving a fish dish. Pesce al Forno con Verdure (Baked Fish and Veg) pairs ideally with **Sauvignon Blanc.**

Flavours: lively, fresh, crisp and fruity.

Bouquet: citrus, white peach, and boxwood with mineral notes.

Formaggio e Frutta (Cheese and Fruit) is kind of delicate lead into the dessert course proper which is coming next. **Moscato d'Asti** is the perfect accompaniment as a sweet Italian white wine.

Flavour: fruity frizzante with orange blossom, honey suckle, pear, Mandarin orange, and Meyer lemon.

Bouquet: peaches, crisp lemons, orange blossoms, and fresh grapes.

Dolce (Sweet) is the real dessert in the Italian meal. **Brachetto d'Acqui** is the sparkling and aromatic wine to serve.

Flavour: sweet, soft, and lightly fizzy.

Bouquet: rose, raspberry, strawberry, and moss.

Caffe coffee or espresso after the meal is accompanied best by the likes of the Tuscan dry Red, Chianti.

Flavour: red Fruits, bitter herbs, smoke, game, and balsamic vinegar.

Bouquet: cherry and plum with savoury notes ad a hint of cedar wood.

Digestivo or Ammazzacaffe (Coffee killer) goes deliciously with **Grappa** which can have varying flavours depending on many variants.

Flavour: soured plums with a honey twist, berry sweetness and caramel tones.

Bouquet: from nutty and crisp to dark chocolate and raisins, and a whole lot of nose in between, depending on the style of Grappa selected.

Sample Menu 2:
Romantic Dinner for Two

Whether it's Valentine's Day, an Anniversary, that pre-proposal meal or just a cosy dinner for two, we have suggestions.

Start with a **crab bisque** accompanied with a rich chardonnay.

Flavour: apple, peach, apricot, pear.

Bouquet: hazelnut, cream and butter.

Main Course: Slow-roasted beef **tenderloin** served with a Spicy **Shiraz**.

Flavour: Cloves, coriander, nutmeg, ginger, cinnamon, cumin, turmeric, white pepper, black pepper, aniseed, and bay leaf.

Bouquet: fruity.

Bring on the sweets in the form of a **chocolate fondue** served with fresh fruits and rounded off with a **pink Prosecco**.

Flavour: pink rose petals and watermelon.

Bouquet: florals, fruitiness, strawberry and cherry

Sample Menu 3:
Summer Picnic

Now that you have the blanket rolled up and the picnic basket filled with salads, crackers, crusty breads, deli meats, meringues, and fresh fruits, let's check on the suitable wines. If you have little people with you, take a long a bottle of chilled sparkling apple or grape juice to allow them the feel of the occasion. In wines, you're looking for light and fruity.

- Chenin Blanc or Pinot Blanc are fruitier, loaded with crisp citrus fruit, and are bright, and acidic.

- Riesling is dry with a crisp acidity and light mineral flavour.

- Rosé wines are floral and fruity and lightly acidic with red fruit, melon, and strawberry qualities just perfect for picnic fare.

- Pinot Noir, a lighter red with either fruity, floral, spicy, or herbal flavours, suited to a variety of picnic options.

- Gamay is another light bodied Red, with black currant, banana, violet, raspberry, and potting soil flavours and a bouquet of iris and peony flowers and fresh cut violets enveloped in raspberry, cherry, and plum.

- Beaujolais is a lighter red with tastes of red berry (cranberry, raspberry, cherry, and red currant), with smoky notes of mushroom and forest floor.

Sample Menu 4:
Amuse-Bouches

This French term literally means mouth amuser. These are served accompanied by a complementary wine as an introduction to the fare that will follow. Amuse Bouches are not quite an appetizer, although they do precede the meal. An Amuse-Bouche is a bite sized teaser of what to expect, and you can serve these up with full-bodied **Burgundy and Merlot**. The fruitiness and subtle bitterness makes a suitable kick off to any meal. It is never unappreciated when **Sparkling Wine** is served upon entry, and this gels perfectly with the concept of Amuse-Bouche. Stick with a dry around the level of brut when it comes to sweetness.

Sample Menu 5:
Family Holiday Feasts (Christmas/Thanksgivings/Cultural Fests)

For a diverse consortium such as will present when the family make up a guest list, you are likely to experience some obstacles, pitfalls and dilemmas. Relax…. or rather, chill! All will be well. It is quite possible that you will have guests who do not like white wine at all. For these, you can feel free to substitute with a rosé or a light red when the dish demands a white. If a red and white is required, but it is not within the budget to go with more than one variety of each, a safe bet is a Chardonnay for the white and Pinot Noir for the red. This white and red option will be fine with most flavours and textures.

Snack platters and Amuse-Bouches comprised of cheese, cured meats, olives, pickles and fig preserve, are great for holiday gatherings or to tide house guests over before the celebratory meal. Focus on Italian wines such as Sangiovese and Pinot Grigio, lending sharp acidity and youthful exuberance to the mix.

For the main meal, Rosé Champagne is simply perfect whether guests are enjoying fatty meats, turkey, duck, or anything in between and on the side. To concentrate more specifically on the turkey, cranberry immediately comes to mind. Choose a wine with cranberry flavour or bouquet, such as Zinfandel. Also recommended for turkey is a bubbly Sparkling Wine or Cabernet. Bordeaux Red wines go splendidly with beef, as does Cabernet. For pork, Merlot or Zinfandel goes well with the obligatory cranberry. Cabernet Sauvignon, Shiraz and Petit Verdot pair well with lamb.

Vegetarians will enjoy pairing their culinary delights with Pinot Noir, Pinot Gris, Chardonnay, Beaujolais, Zinfandel, Merlot and Shiraz. A wide selection to take the panic out of the preparation.

When the diners are fully sated and the dining part of the celebrations are winding down, serve a fairly light, off-dry white wine with the whipped cream and pumpkin pie, or whatever it is you and yours desire as dessert.

Disclaimer

This book contains opinions and ideas of the author and is meant to teach the reader informative and helpful knowledge while being entertaining. The instructions and strategies are possibly not right for every reader and there is no guarantee that they work for everyone. Using this book and implementing the information / recipes therein contained is explicitly your own responsibility and risk. This work with all its contents, does not guarantee correctness, completion, quality or correctness of the provided information. Misinformation or misprints cannot be completely eliminated

Design: Oliviaprodesign

Picture: Mariyana M

Printed in Great Britain
by Amazon

35263685R00066